METAPHYSICAL
DELUSION

In Memoriam

H. R. C.

METAPHYSICAL DELUSION

FRASER COWLEY

PROMETHEUS BOOKS
BUFFALO, NEW YORK

Published 1991 by Prometheus Books

With editorial offices located at 700 East Amherst Street, Buffalo, New York 14215, and distribution facilities located at 59 John Glenn Drive, Amherst, New York 14228.

Library of Congress Cataloging-in-Publication Data

Cowley, Fraser.
    Metaphysical delusion / by Fraser Cowley.
       p. cm.
    Includes bibliographical references and index.
    ISBN 978-0-87975-669-7
    1. Knowledge, Theory of. 2. Belief and doubt. 3. Metaphysics.
I. Title.
BD161.C66 1991
121'.7—dc20
                                                   91-16767
                                                     CIP

Contents

Contents

Introduction

Knowledge and belief are usually taken to be the results of experience, inquiry, inference, hearsay, and practical activity. They are not themselves actions, activities, processes, or events, but more or less lasting states of a person or animal. How then can we be urged to believe or told that we ought to or had better believe something, and how can we say we decided to believe this or that? We often seem to regard belief not as a resultant state, like knowledge, but as some kind of action or activity, as something we can do or not do as we choose. The explanation seems to be this. Beliefs need not be displayed, but when they are it is principally by our doing things that we would not otherwise do. When we are urged to believe something, what is demanded is that we act as if we did, that we do things that could be regarded as displaying the belief, whether we find the thing credible or not.

There are, however, many things people want to believe but do not believe. They have motives to believe—desires, hopes, and fears—but none of the usual sources is sufficient to produce the belief. What they commonly do is to engage in activities, the function of which is not, like inquiry, to determine whether the belief is true, nor merely to insure against the risk of its being true, but just to induce or sustain the belief that it is true.

Consider the words of the Christian creed: "I believe in God the Father Almighty, Maker of Heaven and Earth. . . ." The words are those of a performative utterance, and the act performed in saying them is that of affirming the belief or of confessing the faith. A person may be asked in many contexts whether he believes what he says, that is, whether his *declaration* is sincere. But a person who performs this act of confessing the faith may be asked if his *belief* is sincere. This question is like the question whether a vow, a promise, or a compliment is sincere, as if the act were an act not merely of affirming but of believing. This is belief in the sense of "faith." A mere factual belief arising from the usual sources, whether it is about when the grocer closes or about the composition of the rings of Saturn, could not be sincere or insincere. Only beliefs of faith can.

Few of the actions in which ordinary factual beliefs and knowledge are displayed are simply meant to display them. Where beliefs of faith are concerned, however, many of the acts, actions, and activities, private and public, that ostensibly manifest the belief are meant to do so. They arise from the desire to believe and without them this desire would be unfulfilled. People profess to believe what they desire to believe in order to believe it. People pray for faith as they obviously would not if they had none: "Lord, I believe; Help thou mine unbelief." Faith, unlike merely factual belief, has to be kept up by doing and saying special things to keep it up. The function of these acts and activities is to induce and sustain the belief by displaying and proclaiming it. They are, in effect, acts of believing, whether sincere or insincere. The intent of the act of affirming a credo is not just to make known what one believes and that one believes it, but that it shall be true and that one shall believe it.

If by "disposition" one understands a tendency to do a certain kind of thing or various kinds of things, neither knowledge nor empirical belief are dispositions. But belief in the sense of "faith" is indeed a disposition, the disposition to act in ways that will induce the desired state of mind. Without the desire to believe there is no belief in the sense of "faith." It is strong only as the desire to believe is strong, and the ardor of the acts and activities is that of the desire. The effect of these acts, the resulting state of mind, is then often taken to be evidence for the truth of what is believed and not merely for the efficacy of the activity that constitutes believing it.

At the end of the wager argument, Blaise Pascal's interlocutor says: "Mais . . . je suis fait d'une telle sorte que je ne puis croire. Que voulez-vous que je fasse?" ("But I am so made that I cannot believe. What would you have me do?"). To this Pascal replies:

> Work then, not at convincing yourself by proofs of God, but by diminishing your passions . . . learn from those who were bound like

you and who now wager all they have . . . follow the way by which they began: by acting as if they believed, by taking holy water, by having Masses said, etc. Even naturally, that will make you believe and will tame you . . . I tell you, you will gain by it in this life, and with every step you take on this road, you will see so much certainty of gain, and your risk to be so nullified, that you will know in the end that you have wagered on something certain, infinite, for which you have given nothing.[1]

This final certainty, according to the doctrine, is the supernatural gift of God. What is granted is still faith and not knowledge. The point of Pascal's "naturellement même" ("even naturally") is that the activities of which making the wager consists will have desirable consequences even without this gift. It would hardly do in this context to mention that the gift may not be granted. But is it not hypocrisy to act as if one believed and to profess to believe what one does not believe? Only, it would seem, if there is no desire to believe. Sincerity and fervor are nothing but the strength of the desire.

There are many secondary and derivative motives for religious and metaphysical faith, but the primary and perennial one is, I think, to appease a certain anxiety in a sense distinct from that of "fear." Religions provide a sense of what we are, where we stand, how we ought to live, and of a meaning and purpose in life. Anxiety may be defined negatively as the lack of all that. It arises when some established faith ceases to appease it. But positively it is, I think, the obscure apprehension of our freedom. Where we stand and the meaning or purpose of our lives depend on us. That this should not be so is what we desire and the activities of believing are the expression of that desire. When anxiety arises, it demands appeasement, not analysis, and people who lose one faith commonly seek another.

Pascal does offer an analysis and a direction for its appeasement. A sense of lack and a recurrent ennui and anxiety which no diversion can finally dispel, are, according to him, accounted for by the Christian doctrine of the Fall as by no other, and hence provide not just a motive for faith, but a reason for that faith. There are also what he takes to be reasons of historical fact—these and not the traditional proofs of the existence of God are what he takes to be proofs of God—but they include miracles and the like, which could hardly be so regarded without faith.

In Kierkegaard, by contrast, the distinction of reasons and motives seems to disappear altogether. His central notions of paradox and of subjective truth are, as they stand, incoherent. For reasons that Hume among others expounded, and which were well known to Kierkegaard, no historical inquiry will ever confirm the supernatural parts of the Gospels or the interpretation of the whole. Even if it were easier than it is to establish the core of historical fact, the doctrine of the Incarnation and the Resurrection would not be made more credible. Kierkegaard's conclusion is that historical inquiry, or any kind of factual inquiry, is irrelevant to faith. In his doctrine of subjectivity and subjective truth, the intensity of the belief is flagrantly confounded with the truth of what is believed. The further step is one he cannot take and yet remain a believer: to recognize that faith creates its own objects and its own "truths." The notion of subjective truth is the impossible half-way stage: in so far as subjective truth is *truth*, the objects and propositions about them cannot be faith-dependent, but in so far as it is *subjective*, of course they are just that. One cannot have it both ways. But in Kierkegaard's doctrine one cannot even have it one way. The believer cannot simply regard the objects as imaginary. But if he does not, it can only be because he *will* not: Kierkegaard has left him no factual ground—credibility and probability have nothing to do with faith. His notion of the individual's infinite interest provides no ground for Christian faith but on the contrary presupposes it. All the reasons arise from the commitment, none is prior to it. To make the leap of faith one must, as it were, have made it already. There is no *reason* to make it, but only a motive. If the anxiety were simply dispelled, there would be no motive.

Kierkegaard's polemic against Hegelian philosophy in the *Concluding Unscientific Postscript* may be taken as a polemic against any philosophy that claims or appears to claim to supersede religion, or in which religion is transcended or absorbed as it is in Hegel's philosophical version of Christian eschatology. But the object of Kierkegaard's irony—the unimportance in the Hegelian version of suffering individuals except as tools and instruments in the self-realization of Spirit—is precisely its attraction for many people. In Kierkegaard's derisive characterization, the abstract thinker is a double being, "a fantastic creature who moves in the pure being of abstract thought, and on the other hand, a sometimes pitiful professorial figure which the former deposits, much as one lays down a walking stick."[2] But that is just what many people want—to rise in thought above and beyond themselves. The beauty of it is that thought costs nothing. The system need not be Hegelian. There need not even be a system. Philosophy can be a self-justifying activity, an end in itself, which itself appeases anxiety, though hardly an acute anxiety. What Kierkegaard says of the Hegelian philosophy—"that the thinker's existence contradicts his thought, shows that we are here dealing merely with professions"[3]—is true of many types of philosophy besides that of Hegel. This was already true of doctrinal Christianity.

Kierkegaard in his earlier work *Either-Or* seems in effect to recognize that commitment is practical and that practical reasons arise from commitment and not commitment from reasons. The life of noncommitment he identifies under the name of the Aesthetic. The Ethical, as he describes it, is really the ethical-religious life in the Lutheran tradition. People are primarily committed to such an ethos by birth and upbringing. It is inherited in the same way as any aspect of a common culture and inseparable from a web of practices, institutions, and social relations. It is a religious ethos. Until very recently, most common moralities were, however they might depart from the strict requirements of doctrine.

The recognition that common moralities are historical and not eternal is the first step to the recognition that they exist only by the collective commitment of people to them and have no other foundation. The modern study of ethics and indeed the familiar modern concept of ethics in philosophy arose in part from the desire to replace the religious and specifically Christian foundation with another that would be no less ultimate and universal. In my view, any such foundation is a matter of faith. I take it that there is no such foundation, but whether a well-entrenched common morality can survive without the belief in such a foundation seems to me an open question.

Mythical belief may exist without theological doctrine, and it is mythical belief that is supposed to be inseparable from rites, rituals, and ceremonies. But any faith, doctrinal or not, requires some kind of activity to induce and sustain it, even if it is only or principally verbal. This holds true for philosophical doctrines including many which their authors would not regard as metaphysical. The acts and activities of doctrinal faith belong to a large class that I call in a figurative sense performances, by analogy with an actor's performance of a part or a company's performance of a play. A performance is often given before an audience, present or potential, and is meant to affect the audience, but the performer is also his own audience and affects himself. Unlike a dramatic performance in the literal sense, a performance is not meant to be recognized as a performance by the audience or by the performer. When the performer is aware of what he is doing, he is pretending, feigning, or simulating. The performances I am concerned with are those in which the performer is taken in by his own performance, whether or not others see through it. Obviously a person cannot deceive himself as he can somebody else. To be really deceived, one must have a false belief concerning some matter of fact—one must be mistaken. But in so-called self-deception, one is not mistaken or misled, as one person can be by the words or conduct of another. The unacknowledged intent of the performance is that things shall be and the performer himself shall be as the performance makes out that they are. To acknowledge this intent would be to admit either that they are not so or that there is no reason to believe them to be so, and hence to abandon the performance or lapse into pretense. Doctrinal performances mostly require the complicity of others who take the performance at its face value—without this the performance is apt to collapse—and an institutional and professional framework is often essential. The wrong audience can ruin things—not so much because they cannot understand what is being said as because they do not understand or will not play the game.

There are many performances besides those of doctrinal faith in which the intent is to believe and the actions and words are meant to induce and sustain a belief. Among them are those that Jean-Paul Sartre analyzed, suggestively rather than perspicuously, under the name of bad faith in *Being and Nothingness*. In its ordinary sense bad faith is perfidy, duplicity, or hypocrisy: when a person acts in bad faith it is someone else who is or is meant to be deceived or duped. But in Sartre's sense it is the performer himself. For impromptu everyday performances, there are countless ready-made roles into which we can conveniently slip. Though we do not tell ourselves what we are up to, it does not follow that we always deceive ourselves, nor that these little performances are reprehensible. In the section of *Being and Nothingness* entitled "The 'Faith' of Bad Faith," Sartre gives an analysis of faith which it would be absurd to apply to such performances, but which does apply to performances of the much more elaborate and sophisticated kind that I call doctrinal. The contrast with bad faith is good faith, and if there is a "faith" of bad faith, one might expect there to be a "faith" of good faith too. But it is not clear what that would be. The real contrast with what Sartre describes is not any kind of faith but knowledge and factual belief. What he describes is just faith:

> . . . if the existence of bad faith is very precarious, if it belongs to the kind of psychic structures that we might call "metastable," it presents nonetheless an autonomous and durable form; it can even be the normal aspect of life for a very great number of people. One can live in bad faith, which does not mean one may not have abrupt wakenings of cynicism or good faith, but which implies a constant and particular style of life.[4]

> Bad faith apprehends evidence, but it is resigned in advance not to be satisfied with it, not to be persuaded and transformed into good faith: it is all humility and modesty, it knows quite well, it says, that faith is decision and that after each intuition, it must decide and *will what is the case*. Thus bad faith in its primary project and from the first moment decides the exact nature of its requirements, its whole character is revealed in the resolution it makes *not to demand too much*, to rest satisfied when it is unpersuaded, to force by decision its adherence to uncertain truths. This first project of bad faith is a decision in bad faith on the nature of faith. Let us be clear that this is not a reflective voluntary decision but a spontaneous determination of our being. One slips into bad faith as one falls asleep and one is in bad faith as one dreams. Once this mode of being is achieved, it is as difficult to leave it as to wake oneself up: bad faith is a type of being in the world, like waking or dreaming, which tends to perpetuate itself, although its structure is of the *metastable* type.[5]

As an account of belief in many theological and metaphysical doctrines, including some of Sartre's own, I think this is on the right track. But works of metaphysics are performances of a special literary kind, an edited record, and usually the fruit of many performances. Nothing could be less spontaneous or more deliberate than such doctrines, and many of their authors, far from resolving "not to demand too much and deciding to accept uncertain truths," have ostensibly insisted on rigorous standards of argument. But we have to distinguish the ostensible intent, the intent *within* the performance, from the real intent, the intent *of* the performance. The performance is spontaneous, but everything in it may be deliberate and carefully constructed to accomplish the spontaneous intent and in conformity to its exact requirements. Such performances improve with practice and easily become habitual. A person can become a regular doctrinal performer or believer.

How can one tell whether the profession of a doctrine is a performance? The standard way of telling whether anyone really believes what he professes to believe is to observe his words and actions when he is not professing the belief. But many metaphysical doctrines have the peculiar character that a believer could not fail to talk and act in a way that contradicted his doctrinal professions.

The states that contrast with knowledge and with mundane factual belief are disbelief and doubt or nonbelief. But doctrinal belief has its own negative counterpart—doctrinal doubt or skepticism, which is itself a matter of faith, and, like positive faith, has to be sustained. From skeptical doubt as from positive faith, as Hume said, we "can easily return to our vulgar and natural notions."[6] In my view, we return to what we really do know and believe. A principal function of negative faith or skepticism is precisely to discount common knowledge and belief, our vulgar and natural notions, by putting them in the same boat as faith, to make way for the positive metaphysical doctrine.

Descartes provides a perfect example. His professed ulterior object is certainty, but to that end his first aim must be to doubt. His doubt is intentional, like any faith. And like belief in the sense of "faith," it consists of verbal acts and activities. In the Fourth Meditation Descartes mentions doubting explicitly as a free act of will. Knowledge and error in the performance do not simply result, as real knowledge and error do, from what practical experience and investigation bring or fail to bring to light: they require also the act of will or judgment, of affirmation or denial. What is prescribed in the doctrine is enacted in the performance. As Hobbes pointed out to him, affirmation and denial are matters of will or, as we should say, intentional acts, but whether we affirm or deny that *p* and whether or not we know that *p* are two quite different things.[7] We can lie. The supposed act of judgment that inaugurates true knowledge is a fiction like the act of doubt. Affirmation and denial and abstention from affirming or denying are taken by Descartes to be acts of thought of which the verbal acts are the mere outward expression. "I doubt," "I affirm," and "I deny" in Descartes are really all on a par with "I believe" in the Creed. The essential move in this kind of performance is an act of faith on the nature, not of faith, but of knowledge, belief, doubt, and error.

Meditation is a kind of performance that belongs originally to devotional life. The distinction of inner and outer, soul and body, is assumed in meditation, but the belief in it is sustained only by its enactment in the performance. The subject ostensibly turns within and shuts out the world and the flesh or considers them only from the standpoint of inwardness. Thus in Descartes they are present in the first place only as ideas. His initial aim of detachment from the senses is analogous to the Stoic aim of detachment from passion or desire: the *epecho* or "I abstain" is an epistemic exercise in the one case and an ethical exercise in the other. Practice, with review of previous exercises, is required to improve the performance and ostensibly to overcome the natural and inveterate immersion in the world and the flesh. The intent *within* Descartes' performance is to establish the foundation and the criteria of true knowledge— and of course the existence of God and the real distinction of body and mind. The intent of the performance is that what is affirmed within it shall be true and that we will believe it. If we acknowledged this, the performance would be mere pretense. To be sincere, we must be deceived.

How is such a thing possible? It is accomplished through a use of language that dissociates the metaphysical propositions in the performance from what we really do know or that misconstrues what we know—sometimes both. Instead of distraction—an essential device in Sartre's account of impromptu performances—real knowledge is discounted in metaphysical doctrines quite casually, and with a little practice quite effortlessly, by linguistic disconnection.

When Descartes claims in the Second Meditation that it is not by vision or touch that he knows the wax but only by an inspection of the mind, he remarks on the conflict with vulgar speech and at once brushes it aside: "A man who tries to raise his knowledge beyond the common must be ashamed to draw occasion to doubt from the forms and terms of vulgar speech."[8] Any objection to the doctrine or any conclusion that might be drawn from it in these forms and terms of vulgar speech, the language of common knowledge, is thus ruled out of court: it is not to be acknowledged in the performance. By the same token any doubt of the straight, vulgar, everyday kind is set aside and only the intentional doubt within the performance is to be admitted. But of course anyone, whether he professes the doctrine or not, uses the common terms when he is not professing it. When he is not performing, he talks and acts as if it were not true. The being that sees and feels a piece of wax is neither a human body nor an immaterial mind, but a human being, a man or woman, and what he sees and handles is before his eyes and in his hand. To know the wax is flexible, all he need do is bend it. This is common knowledge— what we all know and, of course, what Descartes knew. The disconnection from vulgar speech is a disconnection from common knowledge—real, practical knowledge of what wax is like. But the threatened *réveil de bonne foi*, or "awakening of good faith" (in Sartre's phrase), has been averted by dismissal of the terms of vulgar speech.

Another awakening threatens in the First Meditation, when Descartes says that if he denied he had a body or that he was seated by the fire in a dressing gown, he would be like those deranged people —*ces insensés*—who, dressed in rags, believe they are kings clothed in velvet or that they have bodies made of glass.[9] What is the difference between these people and Descartes? One difference is that their beliefs are not doctrinal. Another is that they not only proclaim and profess them but to some extent act them out. But they too are apt to have awakenings—they sometimes lapse into behaving as if they did not believe their own claims. Theirs is a kind of individual private faith. The belief that one's body is made of glass is more remarkable than other forms of the belief in transsubstantiation only by its rarity. But such beliefs are really no more remarkable than Descartes' belief that it is not he, the being of flesh and blood, who perceives, but an immaterial being, and that what it perceives is not real things and beings like himself, there in front of him, but ideas. That there are ideas goes without saying. *Cogito* (I think) entails or is synonymous with *Habeo ideas* (I have ideas). But if what one took for horses and cows were ideas, of course one might doubt whether there were any horses or cows and therefore whether one had a body and whether there was a world at all. The belief that there are ideas is a delusion, but a harmless one since there is no conceivable way of acting it out except in the philosophical performance of professing it. The performance alone sustains it. And everybody, the performer included, knows it is a man of flesh and blood who is professing this remarkable doctrine.

A more subtle way than mere dismissal of neutralizing common knowledge is to make out that it, too, or the common language, incorporates an unconscious metaphysical doctrine: common sense metaphysics. But even "common sense" here is a doctrinal expression. What the vulgar call common sense is a practical virtue, by no means universal, which is displayed by things like staying in bed when one has the flu or in not smoking near a gas pump. The heart of common sense in the doctrinal sense, however, is a so-called belief in material objects and their perceptible properties. Again, this is belief in a doctrinal sense. In the vulgar sense there is no such belief. We do not believe in horses. We know there are horses. We see them galloping about or browsing; some people ride them, some breed them, and some bet on them at the races. What we believe in or believe in the existence of, are things which, unlike horses, we do not know there are—beings such as ghosts, fairies, angels, gods, God, and Santa Claus, and last but not least, immaterial minds or souls and ideas.

Take Berkeley. If Berkeley really believed there was no matter, he would believe there were no kinds of matter such as gold, coal, soup, or toffee, nor anything composed of any kind of stuff, not least himself, there being no flesh, blood, or bone. Since he would clearly be deranged, there would be no point in showing him some stuff or in giving him—like Dr. Johnson—a practical demonstration. But Berkeley was not deranged. He did not act out his doctrine and for obvious reasons could not. He did not, and could not, really believe it. The performance of professing it alone sustained his faith. A wakening occurs when he notes how strange it is to say we eat and drink ideas.[10] His response is summed up in the dictum that we should think with the learned and speak with the vulgar.[11] But if we do not think as we speak we are not saying what we think. If we eat and drink, we must be no less composed of matter than what we eat and drink, and there is no doubt that we do eat and drink. To say that Johnson kicked a stone is to speak with the vulgar, but either we mean by "a stone" a lump of stone and by "stone" a kind of hard stuff or we are not saying what we think. Though Berkeley in his doctrine holds that only minds can act and that ideas are inactive or inert, he freely uses transitive action verbs as well as terms for kinds of stuff and things made of stuff, not only when he is *not* professing the doctrine but even when he is.

A sympathetic reader engages in the performance with the author of a metaphysical doctrine. People who offer flat, factual objections are in a sense quite right to do so, but their objections rest on a mistake. The mistake is to suppose that the doctrine professed in the performance is some kind of factual thesis. That is why their objections sometimes provoke knowing smiles. But whereas they are in this respect mistaken, the performers themselves are self-deluded. The difference between Dr. Johnson and Berkeley was not that he knew things and could do things that Berkeley did not know and could not do, such as kicking a stone and knowing he did so. What he did not grasp was that Berkeley sometimes gave performances in which he figured as Philonous, the immaterialist philosopher, and that in giving them he engaged in harmless self-delusion. Berkeley was a subtle, clever performer. Though he knew just as well as Dr. Johnson that he was a man of flesh and blood and not, as Philonous in the performance was, a mind attended by a congeries of ideas, when he played Philonous he played him so well that he was taken in by his own performance.

The ambition of some older metaphysics and theology was to provide an account of the world and of a more than mundane reality encompassing it and thus to know where we stood. Modern metaphysics begins with a questioning of the mundane without parallel except in ancient skepticism. The task of epistemology, as it came later to be called, is ostensibly to overcome skepticism. But skepticism itself rests on a set of dogmas and assumptions which are themselves metaphysical. Far from being put in suspense until these problems are dealt with, metaphysical doctrine is embodied in the problems themselves. The problems of the Self and of the External World arise equally from the dogma of ideas. The problem of the Self has nothing to do with the referents of personal pronouns or names. It is a problem of the same kind as the problem of God's existence and his nature. Descartes proceeds from the proof of the former to the proof of the latter and thence by a proof of the divine veracity, to the proof of the existence of the "external" world.

The migration of metaphysics from the yonder to the hither side of the world and the retreat within had a strong motive. After the discovery that there was no *there* up there and the consequent sus-

picion that there might be no hereafter hereafter, many people clung
to the hope that the answer to the question "Is this all?" was not
what they feared it might be. But if there were reasons for doubting, not just whether this was all, but whether there was really all
this, there might be hope still. *Reculer pour mieux sauter* was the
idea and the most spectacular leap was Descartes' from "I am" to
"God is." But the silence of the infinite spaces came to be taken
for granted; natural philosophy forged ahead like so many other things;
life for some people became less like a vale of tears; and since the
hereafter was as much a matter of fear as of hope and in some versions rather more, it seemed to some people that it would not be
such a bad thing if this were all. One of them was Hume. But if
he saw no need to *mieux sauter*, why did he bother to *reculer*? The
same may be asked of many later philosophers.

A strong doctrinal tradition imposes itself and its problems on
later generations. Though their preoccupations and motives may be
very different and though they might be glad to be quit of those
problems, such is the power of the established terms of discourse
that sometimes they cannot see how. The doctrine that, in Hume's
words, "no external object can make itself known to the mind immediately, and without the interposition of an image or perception,"[12]
from which skepticism and immaterialism arose, was accepted by
people whose philosophies were otherwise quite different, by materialists such as Priestley and Diderot as well as by Hume. Whether
a philosopher makes anything of it depends on his motives and what
use he has for it. Priestley and Diderot had no time for it and no
use for it. But Hume had a use for it. It provided the negative basis
for his positive secular faith in the nonrational, permanent, and
irresistible principles of human nature, which do and ought to pre-
vail, since beyond them lies nothing but an "ocean of doubt, un-
certainty, and contradiction."[13] Refusing the Cartesian or any other
leap, he sought to found the principles of knowledge and of morals
in these *de facto* principles and to show that these are and ought
to be ultimate. Security was to be found in antimetaphysics, in skepticism itself, and victory grasped from the jaws of defeat. Human
nature was the metaphysical rock or, if not that, the impassible bar-
rier beyond which it made no sense to speak of going. The advantage of this position is clearly on the side of his moral and political
doctrine. The anxiety arising from the threat of moral relativism and

subjectivism is appeased by the claim that the moral sentiments and their objects are no less natural and universal than the belief in the material world, than which obviously nothing could be more secure, though it is entirely unfounded and rests on a kind of "fallacy and illusion."[14]

Though the intent of many eighteenth-century philosophers was to replace a theological anthropology with a natural anthropology, emulating the revolution in natural philosophy and cosmology, it is an understatement to say that the resulting doctrines of human nature were far more like theology than like physics. Epistemology, ethics, and politics were alike founded on dogmas, and the circularity, the question-begging, and the persistent tendency in case of dilemmas to try to have things both ways—with which theology had long been reproached—were no less characteristic of secular metaphysics.

There are fairly simple and glaring objections to all such doctrines and for that reason they always have to be done over again in new performances which cannot just repeat but must at least appear to innovate. But problems arising within such doctrines are perennial to the same extent as the dogmas. Trying to solve them is like trying to flatten the bubbles in an air-tight bag: they merely shift about. Argument and counterargument are really about where in the bag it is better to have the bubbles. When the dogmas incorporated in the terms of the doctrine are brought to light, however, it only remains to discard the whole bag. But people do not readily abandon dogmas, on which their elucubrations have long proceeded. They have invested too much of themselves to be willing at last just to burst the bag. In this century, among others, Wittgenstein, Austin, and Ryle seemed to bid us burst a number of bags. But to the sound of bubbles expiring, a new bag was being puffed up: the so-called philosophy of language. Its problems have the mark of truly metaphysical problems, that of being problems only in the peculiar terms in which they are stated and of being insoluble in these terms. Many are old problems of epistemology in the new bag. Thus we need not lose our inheritance nor any investment we have ourselves made. For every bubble in the old bag we get at least one in the new. The shift from the theory of knowledge to the philosophy of language proves to be no revolution, but just what was needed to save the *ancien régime* from dissolution at the hands of the *sans-culottes*.

The obstacles to countless doctrines are just commonplace truths that everyone knows, and unless one gets round them one cannot even begin the performance. Hence the use of doctrinal terms or familiar terms with a special doctrinal sense is indispensable. Doctrinal claims are sometimes treated as if they were themselves commonplace truths or followed trivially from such truths. Thus the opening paragraph of W. V. Quine's *Ontological Relativity* runs:

> We are prone to talk and think of objects. Physical objects are the obvious illustration when the illustrative mood is on us, but there are also all the abstract objects, or so there purport to be: the states and qualities, numbers, attributes, classes. We persist in breaking reality down somehow into a multiplicity of identifiable and discriminable objects, to be referred to by singular and general terms. We talk so inveterately of objects that to say we do so seems almost to say nothing at all; for how else is there to talk?[15]

Who ever thought a state like knowledge or belief, or a quality like red, or an activity like running was an object? Who ever thought we had to break down reality into cows, sheep, horses, grass, etc.? Quine and many other philosophers did. Those who know Quine's metaphysical doctrine will find an important part of it already in that first paragraph. The end is in the beginning. It is the exordium in a performance of faith, metaphysical faith.

Another and perhaps more commonplace example is this. The fact that we see and hear and have thoughts, feelings, and intentions is taken by many philosophers to entail that there is a special class of events, mental events, of a radically different kind from physical events. A counterdoctrine—feeding from the hand it is biting, as counterdoctrines do—maintains that these events are identical with certain kinds of physical events in the brain. Well, they must be identical or not, must they not? So you're either a physicalist or a mentalist, aren't you? Come now, let's have no shilly-shallying!

For the transmission of metaphysical doctrines and the instruction of new performers, the move from the commonplace to the doctrinal has to be made. In initiating new adepts, old adepts reinitiate themselves and renew their faith by a return to the sources. Plato's early dialogues, Berkeley's *Three Dialogues*, and Russell's *Problems of Philosophy* are works that provide a smooth passage from the familiar to the fantastic and are therefore excellent introductions to philosophy.

When metaphysical doctrines fall from favor, it is not because they have been refuted or because insurmountable objections have at last become apparent. In most cases, quite damning objections are apparent from the start. In at least one case, Plato's, they were apparent to the author himself, and in another, Descartes', the most damaging objections to his principal work of metaphysics were published with it. Doctrines suffer eclipse rather because they have come to seem tedious, antiquated, or futile. People lose their faith. Interest shifts away with changes in the social and material conditions of life, with advances in knowledge, and with changes in practices and institutions and in the desires, hopes, and fears that people have. But revivals are always possible. We have seen State of Nature theory revived from the dead. Many dead doctrines have an afterlife as historical monuments or archetypes, serving to provide an honorific ancestry for later ones that are open to the same crippling objections. This perennity of interest is sometimes taken to show that there must, after all, be something in them. What it shows if anything is that there must be something in *us* that they should prove attractive in different historical contexts. But though the fundamental motive of faith is the same, the secondary and derivative ones may differ widely, and it is far from easy sometimes to see what the appeal of a particular doctrine was at a particular time. One of the functions of metaphysical doctrines is to serve as ultimate justifications or sanctions for attitudes, practices, and aims. But not all of them do it directly through ethical doctrines. Some issues and arguments have the air of being what is called technical, though in fact much more central concerns hinge on them, and the problem is to show the connections.

Many theological doctrines could surely not have survived without a church and clergy whose interest and very existence required their continued propagation. I do not say clerics were insincere or cynical. On the contrary, their interest, material and spiritual, clearly lay in sincerity. In a similar way, many secular philosophical doctrines could not have survived even for a short time without teachers of philosophy whose interest and existence as teachers depended upon their continued promulgation. Of course there are big differences. Philosophy is but one among many academic disciplines and of others similar things can be said. The wilder kind of metaphysics seems to have migrated to other departments such as English literature and computer science. In place of one orthodox doctrine and discipline, philosophy has several quasi-orthodoxies—various conceptual systems within which various doctrinal games may be played. To enter the profession one must play one or more of these recognized games. And this intellectual investment and professional commitment ensures the survival and continuity of the games. One effect of professionalism and careerism is to reduce the polemical and combative character of philosophical writings. In this as in other professions dog does not eat dog; but nowhere is bland ecumenism so pervasive.

The advance of physical science renders many doctrines untenable, not so much by refuting their quasifactual theses, which can perfectly well be done without physical science, as by the contrast it provides in being tied to empirical, practical test and its evident independence of anyone's motives. The kind of metaphysics I am principally concerned with, empiricism, has perhaps more than any other sought to accommodate physical science and to ally itself with it. But what it actually does is to save itself by making metaphysics out of science as well as common knowledge.

The ploy goes back to a defense of Berkeley that he never thought of, and that might make him turn in his grave. It is not too much to say that empiricist metaphysics got from it a whole new lease of life or bag of bubbles. According to this defense, Berkeley's language is simply different and no conclusion in vulgar terms can be drawn from premises in his. It therefore does not follow from his doctrine of ideas either that we eat and drink ideas or that we do not eat and drink at all. A language is itself a conceptual system or theory and from premises in one language no conclusion follows in another. This thesis squares neatly with the much older doctrine that so-called commonsense realism or, as Hume calls it, the popular *system*, is a metaphysical theory. Generalized and applied to different natural languages as well as to scientific theories, the thesis issues in one direction in the Quinean doctrine of objects as posits, of ontological commitment, and of indeterminacy of translation. To make the commitment or espouse the faith of our choice, we must first keep the options open. To this end, we must reject translation understood in the vulgar way as saying the same thing in different words, or expressing the same concepts or propositions in different terms. A language is itself a conceptual system or theory of reality, not a different thing but the same thing. To translate from one language into another is therefore to read the latter theory into the former. Indeterminacy of translation arises from the fact that there is no criterion of identity by which we can say that we have said the same thing in two languages or even, to press the matter, in two different ways in one language. If there were such a thing as the same thing—the same proposition—it would be a putative spook behind the scenes, a mental entity, and unworthy of scientific consideration.

In fact, there was never any such thing as a Berkeleyan or phenomenalist language, but only some few terms that had no use but to expound the doctrine and whose function was to disconnect it from common knowledge and put it beyond straight refutation. The problem is not, and never was, one of translation. The problem is just to determine by their examples what Berkeley took to be an idea and what other philosophers took to be a sense datum, and what they meant by such expressions as "immediate" and "the senses." It is quite easy to do this and hence to show that perception and objects of perception are systematically misdescribed in these doctrines. Phenomenalism treats the way an object looks at a certain distance, at a certain angle, and in a certain light as being itself an object, an immediate object or raw datum, and how it looks from any other angle as another object. Thus, what appears or is perceived is taken to be an appearance and not, for example, a horse or cow. Treating the looks as objects is half the game; the other half is their assimilation to sensations, of which the paradigm is pain. To recognize this is to see that the doctrine is false. The key terms serve only to disconnect the doctrine from what we know—that what is visibly one and the same thing of constant size, shape, and color, looks different from different angles and distances and in different lights. The linguistic defense recognizes that the key terms are important, but not why they are important—that they carry a doctrine that can be readily stated without them and then seen to be false. The defense retains in fact an essential assumption in common with Berkeley— that there are immediate data—but it simply holds that different languages or conceptual systems impose different structures on them or objectify them in different ways. Since Kant lurks in the background of this kind of doctrine, I dub it linguistic transcendentalism. It is an essential part of Quine's physicalism, Wilfrid Sellars's scientific realism, J. J. C. Smart's materialism, and Michael Dummett's Fregeanism. There is no reason why it should not be used in the service of idealism. All the options are open and everyone is free to make his ontological commitments or profess the metaphysical faith of his choice.

The case I take for special study is Quine's. The doctrines he professes in his performances, if taken as factual theses about language, are mostly false and can be shown to be false no less easily than Berkeley's doctrines concerning perception. But according to linguistic transcendentalism this could never be shown, for exactly the same reason as it could never be shown that Berkeley's doctrine is false. The linguistic defense applies no less to doctrines concerning language, to syntactic and semantic terms and to any system of parsing, however perverse, than it does to Berkeley's doctrine concerning perception. Since according to it objects are posits tied to terms of a language, truth is relative to a language, and this includes truths about language; they cannot be literally denied in any other language or meta-language. To anyone who rejects linguistic transcendentalism this is of course false, but in taking it to be a factual thesis we make the same mistake as Dr. Johnson made regarding Berkeley's immaterialism. It is a factual thesis only within the performance, but not without. Just as Berkeleyan apples are not really apples nor the Bishop of Cloyne an immaterial mind, so Quinean truth is not really truth.

Something like indeterminacy of translation has often been thought to characterize metaphysical statements and this is cognate with the problem of knowing how they could be tested and confirmed or falsified. Does "No matter" entail "No toffee"? Does "Time is unreal" entail "We are not really getting any older"? To keep the metaphysical options open we must not answer yes. But the plain answer to these questions is yes, and since there *is* lots of toffee at the corner shop and we *are* getting older, both metaphysical statements are false. The problem is not one of translation, but just of finding the moves in the arguments that lead to the metaphysical statements. Many of Berkeley's are easy to spot. "But is not the most vehement and intense degree of heat a very great pain?" asks Philonous in the first dialogue. The answer is no. A great heat can be painful or cause pain—if you are too close to the source—but it is not a pain. Feeling the heat from something hot is not the same thing as being hot or feeling hot. There is nothing wrong with Berkeley's language. He simply treats many qualities and states of things as if they were sensations like pain, and they are not. He could do without the term "idea." All of Berkeley's arguments are based on a prior sensationalism that was shared by many other philosophers, who therefore could not refute him even when they would. The root of the trouble is not the *idea* idea but the *sensation* idea, the first article of his metaphysical faith. There is nothing wrong with Quine's language either. What is wrong is his doctrine that what we have to go on, and all we have to go on, is the stimulation of our nerve endings, that objects are posits of a language or theory, that a language thus embodies ontological commitments, and that the task of parsing is to expose them. His metaphysical parsing or analysis of English sentences is analogous to Berkeley's analysis of perception and objects of perception.

"We talk so inveterately of objects that to say we do so seems almost to say nothing at all; for how else is there to talk?" The parsing in the performance is faithful to this metaphysical commitment. A term like "envy" in subject position in a sentence is an abstract singular term and its referent or purported referent an abstract object. But envy being, as everyone knows, a type of trait or disposition that people have, it follows that all envious people have this abstract object. This is no less strange than the idea that we eat and drink ideas or sensations. Quine does not remark on it as Berkeley does in the parallel case. If he wanted to use the linguistic defense, he might say that his language is simply different from ours and that no such conclusion in our language follows from premises in his. It therefore no more follows from his doctrine that envious, honest, beautiful, or witty people have diverse abstract objects than it does from Berkeley's that we eat and drink ideas.

It is on Quine's metaphysical parsing that his notion of a suitably regimented and purged language of science is based. And the principal victims of the purge are what he calls abstract objects and mentalistic terms. But the purged language is really just his physicalist doctrine, as the alleged Berkeleyan language is really just Berkeley's immaterialist doctrine. There is no such language in either case.

For countless practical purposes, Quine agrees, we are condemned to use all the common idioms that we reject philosophically, to "switch Muses" when it suits our book. But we need never fear that we contradict our doctrinal professions by our ordinary words and deeds. Thus we have a metaphysical justification for talking out of both sides of our mouths or for not letting our right hands know what our left hands are doing. Though exponents of theological and metaphysical doctrine have always done this, no other has so thoroughly made the need to do so a part of his own doctrine or justified it on the ground that *cosí fan tutti.*

What I call a duplicity thesis is an account within a doctrine of why we are bound, whether or not we espouse it, to talk and act as if it were not true, and why if we do espouse it we cannot but be two-faced. A duplicity thesis is the false colors under which self-delusion sails within the self-deluding doctrine. A classic example is the explanation in Christian doctrine of why believers commonly act as if they did not believe a word of it, and why they are on the whole no more remarkable for virtue than other people. The reason is that Original Sin still blinds and renders heedless even those who have heard the Gospel and accept it; their depravity itself demonstrates the need of prayer, repentance, and redemption by God's grace, just as the doctrine says. Hume remarks at one point of ordinary Christian believers: "I ask if these people really believe what is inculcated on them, and what they pretend to affirm; and the answer is obviously in the negative."[16] But his question concerning these people and their professed doctrine may be asked equally of him and his. He has his own duplicity thesis, an account within his doctrine of why we talk and act as if there were no such things as those "internal and perishing existences,"[17] though what we take to be real things or bodies are, according to his doctrine, just such things.

Quine's doctrine seems to stand in need of just such a thesis and at first sight might even seem to have one. According to it, all objects are posits tied to terms of a language and truth is relative to a language. But people in fact treat posits as real things, independent of any language, and truths about them as simply true. Quine admits a difference of standpoint—the standpoint internal to a language and the standpoint external to it. But according to linguistic transcendentalism there is no standpoint external to any language or theory, and this thesis must itself be relative to a language or theory. So a duplicity thesis is ruled out.

No one should think it unseemly or insulting to look for the motives for metaphysical doctrines. Intellectual honesty is not just common honesty or a matter of common morality. Delusion goes deep. It is not mere pretense, least of all cynical pretense, any more than religious faith. Nor is it merely individual. Every doctrine is a synthesis and development of earlier ones in a common tradition and the fruit of a long development. The appeasement of anxiety by faith is not in itself and in general to be deplored. That depends on the faith and what it justifies or sanctions in practice. No one hesitates to examine the motives for many political, economic, and military doctrines, which are no less matters of faith. Since people can actually try to put them into practice and the test of belief in them is the willingness to put them into practice, they can be very much more alarming. But an interesting question is that of the relation of metaphysical doctrines to these. It is far from being direct or obvious. The closest connection is via ethical doctrines. In a future work, I will take as examples Hume's and some later doctrines of justice. But here I try to show some of the moral and political ramifications of Quine's philosophy of language and science.

Unless one first realizes that a doctrine is not just false but known to be false, one will have no reason to be interested in the motives people have for professing and "believing" it. Much of the first part of this work is therefore devoted to attempting to show resistant readers that some classic doctrines they profess, or profess to find weighty or impressive, are false—and that they know it. Some of the arguments I use are old ones freshened up, and some are new. But in view of what I take to be the nature of faith, I do not suppose they will always have the desired effect. Faith is faith in spite of everything.

NOTES

(Abbreviated references in these and all notes are to editions listed fully in the bibliography.)

1. *Pensées*, p. 116.
   Travaillez donc, non pas à vous convaincre par l'augmentation des preuves de Dieu, mais par la diminution de vos passions . . . apprenez de ceux qui ont été lieś comme vous, et qui parient maintenant tout leur bien . . . suivez la manière par où ils ont commencé: c'est en faisant tout comme s'ils

croyaient, en prenant de l'eau bénite, en faisant dire des messes, etc. Naturellement même, cela vous fera croire et vous abêtira . . . Je vous dis que vous y gagnerez en cette vie; et qu'à chaque pas que vous ferez dans ce chemin, vous verrez tant de certitude de gain, et tant de néant de ce que vous hasardez, que vous connaîtrez à la fin que vous avez parié pour une chose certaine, infinie, pour laquelle vous n'avez rien donné.

2. *Concluding Unscientific Postscript*, trans. Swenson and Lowrie (Princeton, N.J.: Princeton University Press, 1941), p. 268.

3. Ibid., p. 269.

4. Jean-Paul Sartre, *L'Etre et le Néant* (Paris: Coll. TEL Gallimard, 1976; originally published 1943), p. 88.

. . . si l'existence de la mauvaise foi est fort précaire, si elle appartient à ce genre de structures psychiques qu'on pourrait appeler "méta-stables," elle n'en présente pas moins une forme autonome et durable; elle peut même être l'aspect normal de la vie pour un très grand nombre de personnes. On peut vivre dans la mauvaise foi, ce qui ne veut pas dire qu'on n'ait de brusques réveils de cynisme ou de bonne foi, mais ce qui implique un style de vie constant et particulier.

5. Ibid., pp. 108-109.

La mauvaise foi saisit des évidences, mais elle est d'avance résignée à ne pas être remplie par ces évidences, à ne pas être persuadée et transformée en bonne foi: elle se fait humble et modeste, elle n'ignore pas, dit-elle, que la foi est décision, et qu'après chaque intuition, il faut décider et *vouloir ce qui est*. Ainsi la mauvaise foi dans son projet primitif, et dès son surgissement, décide de la nature exacte de ses exigences, elle se dessine tout entière dans la résolution qu'elle prend de *ne pas trop demander*, de se tenir pour satisfaite quand elle sera mal persuadée, de forcer par décision ses adhésions à des vérités incertaines. Ce projet premier de mauvaise foi est une décision de mauvaise foi sur la nature de la foi. Entendons bien qu'il ne s'agit pas d'une décision réfléchie et volontaire, mais d'une détermination spontanée de notre être. On se met de mauvaise foi comme on s'endort et on est de mauvaise foi comme on rêve. Une fois ce mode d'être réalisé, il est aussi difficile d'en sortir que de se réveiller: c'est que la mauvaise foi est un type d'être dans le monde,

comme la veille ou le rêve, qui tend par lui-même à se perpé-
tuer, encore que sa structure soit du type *métastable*.

6. *Treatise*, p. 216.

7. Descartes, *Oeuvres Philosophiques*. Tome II, Objections III, 13,
p. 125.

8. Ibid., *Méditation Seconde*, p. 427. "Un homme qui tâche d'élever
sa connaissance au delà du commun, doit avoir honte de tirer des occasions
de douter des formes et des termes de parler du vulgaire . . ."

9. Ibid., *Première Méditation*, p. 406.

10. *The Principles of Human Knowledge*, par. 38, p. 82.

11. Ibid., par. 51, p. 89.

12. *Treatise*, p. 239.

13. *Enquiry*, p. 103.

14. *Treatise*, p. 189.

15. W. V. Quine, *Ontological Relativity* (New York: Columbia University Press, 1969), p. 1.

16. *Treatise*, p. 114.

17. Ibid., p. 194.

Part One

Some Classic Delusions

1

The Myth of Ideas

For Descartes the necessary and sufficient condition of true knowledge beyond elementary truths of logic and mathematics, is that we can demonstrate that we know, and how we know, what we claim to know. Failing this test, we do not really know something even when by ordinary practical tests we do and have no reason to doubt it. Such a doctrine must start by providing some reason to doubt that we do know such things. But Descartes does much more than that. He introduces a dogma or assumption in the light of which practical tests could not only never be conclusive but could not count at all, and we should have no reason even to believe what by ordinary standards we certainly do know. This assumption, for which he offers no justification or defense, is that ideas exist, that we have ideas, and that some of them are images or representations of various kinds of things. To see a thing of a certain kind, a horse for example, would, according to his doctrine, be at least to have an idea or image of a thing of that kind. The question then is whether any such thing exists independently of the idea of it, and if it does, to what extent the idea is a true idea of it; that is, how close the resemblance is. The doctrine of ideas provides no reason to conclude from the idea of a horse that there is any such thing as a horse, any more than a picture of a fabulous creature provides any reason to believe there is any such creature; and Descartes gives his analysis of the piece of wax before he has attempted to establish that there is any such thing independent of our ideas of it. To establish that there is, requires proof of the existence of God and of the divine veracity. Nothing less would do. But, as we shall see, not even that would do.

At the beginning of the Third Meditation, Descartes mentions as one of his former opinions "that there were objects outside of me from which these ideas proceeded, and to which they were entirely similar."[1] And his final revised view is that they are indeed similar, but not entirely similar. The objects here are material objects like pieces of wax or horses. It seems hardly possible that he regarded this as the naive, natural opinion, since no one who did not have the notion of an idea as an image could possibly hold this opinion. But could anyone who did have that notion possibly hold this opinion? If the idea of a horse were entirely similar to a horse, it would at least be composed of some sort of stuff and might be expected to have solid hooves, to eat grass, to gallop about, and to snort or whinny like a horse. And though the idea of a dragon could not be like a dragon, there being no dragons, it would be like the idea of a horse in being composed of matter, though unlike that of a horse in being scaly, fire-breathing, and ferocious. The same would go for all the ideas of material things and of their properties and interactions that occur, in Descartes' account, in dreams. If any of them were like any material object outside of us, or had the qualities of any such object, it would have to be a material object. For there is no doubt that that is what we take the things we see and touch to be, and therefore what in Descartes' account we must take the ideas to be ideas of. Descartes in fact takes an idea of this kind to be an impression on a sensorium in the brain. That we should have corporeal semblances of horses galloping and whinnying in our brains is so incredible that almost all of Descartes' successors preferred to regard ideas as immaterial, as so-called *mental* images. But mental images are really no better. If they are at all like real material things, having size and shape, being light or heavy, hard or soft, how can they fail to be material? And if they are immaterial, having no size and shape, neither light nor heavy, hard nor soft, how can they be like any material thing? Before any appeal to the divine veracity, the problem is what the divine veracity would be required to guarantee.

Not all ideas in Descartes' account are images or pictures; some commentators have been driven to suggest that even in the case of ideas of bits of wax or horses he does not really mean images. But

there is nothing else he can mean. Only if they were corporeal semblances—and movies at that—on the sensorium would the notion
make sense, however incredible that would be. And that could
obviously not be known before the existence of bodies was established. But that there are ideas is an assumption on which Descartes'
whole argument rests as much as it rests on the *Cogito*, before he
has proved the existence of any material thing. To assume we know
there are ideas we must assume we know what ideas are, what "idea"
means. But it is clear that we do not. The notion of an idea in Descartes and his successors is fraught with perplexity like all the central notions of theology and metaphysics. But that notion is assumed
to be clear and the perplexity is instead foisted upon all the ordinary epistemic notions of knowledge, belief, doubt, experience, ex-
periment, discovery, and so on. The dogma of ideas, with or without
the complementary dogma of the immaterial mind, is the fundamental dogma of skepticism; without the problem of skepticism, epistemology as it is traditionally conceived would hardly exist.

The problem of immaterial ideas that are supposed to resemble
material things is inseparable from the problem of what it is that
has them. When Hobbes asked Descartes what the thing that thinks
is, Descartes' only reply was in effect "a thinking thing." Hobbes
correctly pointed out that this was no answer. If one replied to the
question what the thing is that runs or eats with "the running thing"
or "the eating thing," this would be at best a poor joke. The proper
answer would be something like "a rabbit" or "a horse." One of Descartes' terms for the mind or thing that thinks is "the understanding." But it is no more enlightening to say it is the understanding
that thinks or understands—or the will that wills.[2] It is because no
one has ever done any better than Descartes with the question of
what a mind is that dualism had to shift from the mind or thinking
thing to mental states, events, and processes. This makes it pretty
lopsided. Whereas the physical states are states of a body, and the
physical events and processes are events and processes in a body,
the body being clearly the thing, prudence forbids anyone who realizes that Hobbes did floor Descartes to say that the mental ones
are in or of a mind. So they are left dangling. But it is essential
to many metaphysical performances not to regard a knock-out as
a knock-out. If "mind" were synonymous with "thinking thing," there
is a simple answer to the question what it is: a human being. Des-

cartes has to pretend in his replies to several objections that, until
he has established the real distinction of body and mind, no possibility is closed off. But this one clearly is, by the mere use of the
term "mind" or "esprit."

Without skepticism with regard to the senses, there would have
been no problem of knowledge and no problem of the "external"
world as these have been understood by generations of philosophers.
How did it arise? The universal and primary opinion of all men that
perceptible material things are independent of any perception of them,
says Hume, "is soon destroyed by the slightest philosophy, which
teaches us, that nothing can ever be present to the mind, but an
image or perception, and that the senses are only the inlets, through
which these images are conveyed, without being able to produce any
immediate intercourse between the mind and the object . . . no man,
who reflects, ever doubted, that the existences, which we consider,
when we say, *this house* and *that tree*, are fleeting copies or representations of other existences, which remain uniform and independent."[3] From this arises the skeptical problem: "The mind has never
anything present to it but the perceptions, and cannot possibly reach
any experience of their connection with objects. The supposition of
such a connection is, therefore, without any foundation in reasoning."[4]

It does not follow from any account of the stimulation of our
nerve endings and neurocerebral reactions that there are such images, nor that the things we actually encounter in all our practical
dealings are not real physical things that exist quite independently
of us. But if we assume that a person consists of two things, a body
and a mind, it is a natural conclusion. A mind, unlike a body, does
not physically confront real things themselves at a certain distance,
but can at best have perceptions or images caused by, or occurring
on the occasion of, bodily processes. Except in Descartes' account
where apparently the mind does confront real things in the head,
it is assumed that, a mind being itself immaterial, only immaterial
things can be present to it. The ordinary verbs of perception apply
to human beings and a thing is present when it is within sight or
reach of such a being and absent when it is elsewhere. So long as
the subject is taken to be a human being or an animal, himself an
object of perception, his objects of perception are all the usual things
—visible, audible, and tangible, that human beings perceive and manipulate. Objects of imagination are likewise material things and even

when they are fictitious, they are fictitious material things. But if it is a mind that perceives and what is present to it either in perception or imagination is immaterial, what can this be but a perception, image, or idea? Though in any so-called mental image of a horse, the object is not the image but a horse, the image, idea, or perception is in this doctrine taken to be itself an immediate object, the distinction between the image of the object and the object of the image drops out, and we end up with an immaterial horse. Of course we still speak of an image or idea *of* a horse, but if the image were a picture of a horse as this suggests, the case would be no better, for the notion of an immaterial picture of a horse is neither more nor less absurd than the notion of an immaterial horse. An idea, says Berkeley, can be like nothing but another idea. A material thing, say I, can be like nothing but another material thing. There is no such thing in a mind or out of it as an immaterial horse.

If the representative theory had not been assumed to follow from the causal, no other argument for immediate images or perceptions would have carried any weight. But the doctrine that what is present to the mind is only perceptions forbids any knowledge of the causes of the perceptions. The kind of argument that Hume, and of course Berkeley, offer for the mind-dependent perceptions or images ostensibly makes no appeal to their causation. Hume gives one such argument in the same context as the passages I have just quoted: "The table which we see, seems to diminish, as we remove further from it: but the real table, which exists independent of us, suffers no alteration: it was, therefore, nothing but its image, which was present to the mind."[5] How a table looks at different distances is here taken to be an image "present to the mind." But how it looks is not an image of the table, nor does the table seem to diminish. Things like tables, in one sense of "look," look smaller the further away they are and larger the nearer they are; if they did not, they would not be seen as being of constant size but as shrinking or expanding. To appear is of course to be perceived under particular conditions. But what appears is not therefore an appearance or image but the real material thing, a table. Assume that it is not the real thing that appears, that the mind has never anything present to it but perceptions, that it is perceptions or appearances that appear, that these are the immediate objects, and of course it follows that the supposition of any connection with real things is "without any foundation in reasoning."

Hume and Berkeley both showed that if one accepts the arguments for the mind-dependence of so-called secondary qualities, precisely analogous arguments oblige one to accept the mind-dependence of primary qualities too—size or extension is a case in point. But again it seems highly doubtful whether any of these arguments would have carried any weight without the causal theory. Since this argument is still with us, we may put it in modern terms. The light rays entering the eye are distinguished simply by wavelength and frequency. They are not colored. Perception of color is caused by stimulation of the cones which are sensitive to light of different wavelengths; some color differences correspond to light of various wavelengths, but color itself has no independent existence. This is a plausible argument and it is difficult at first to see what is wrong with it. The Berkeleyan and Humean types of argument, however, are much less so, and if they were not thought somehow to support this one they would surely not be thought so at all. To show this, let us put Berkeley's procedure in reverse and instead of moving from secondary qualities to primary, as he does in the first Dialogue, move from primary to secondary and thence back to physics.

Suppose we see a pyramidal object at some distance with the triangular faces at an angle of 45 degrees, but on a closer approach we find it is a pile of cubical boxes, all the faces of which are either vertical or horizontal. We then look at the edge of one of the boxes and observe it to be dead straight. But taking a strong glass we see numerous irregular indentations. Now a principal type of argument for the mind-dependence of primary qualities and therefore of our supposed material objects is that the contrary assumption would require us to ascribe incompatible characteristics to one and the same thing. But it is clear in this case that we do not. Everyone knows that a pile of boxes can very well form a pyramid and that from a distance we may make out the pyramid but not the boxes, and likewise that an edge which is straight overall may be irregular in detail. The pile of boxes is pyramidal and each box is cubical, the faces of the pyramid are at 45 degrees, the sides of the boxes are vertical or horizontal. The whole edge is straight, but little bits are crooked. Those who do not want to go the whole hog with Berkeley's view sometimes say that descriptions are relative to a standpoint.

Certainly, whatever we perceive or think about, we always have some standpoint, perceptual, practical, or theoretical. But it does not follow that descriptions are relative to a standpoint in the sense of not being true or false of independent things as they are in themselves. It just follows that it is only from various standpoints that we can attend to and get at different things as they are in themselves, the pyramid of boxes or the boxes, the whole edge or short stretches. We pick out what to describe, but what we describe, what the descriptions are true or false of, and whether they are true or false, is quite independent of us.

Consider now two analogous cases from which it is customary to draw momentous conclusions. A mauve patch of color proves on closer examination to consist of small red and blue dots: and in Berkeley's familiar example, a red spot of blood under the microscope is seen to consist of pink spots surrounded by white. The conclusion is that since nothing can be both mauve *and* red and blue, or both red *and* pink and white, color is not a real property of things but is mind-dependent. There may be other and better arguments for that conclusion, but this one is a dud. None of the things that are red and blue is the same as the thing that is mauve. The mauve patch may be made up of red and blue dots, just as the pyramid may be made up of boxes. Only someone who was already convinced on some other ground that color was not a real property of things would be impressed by the argument. Anyone who adopts the philosophical convention of calling color a quality is already softened up. What is often meant by "a quality" in philosophical writings is what Ayer, Goodman, and others call a *quale*. A *quale* is not a property of things, so what can it be but a sensation or something in us? But the color of a colored surface is a property of the surface matter. Note what is meant by "a property." Water boils at 100°C. This ascribes a property to water. It does not entail that any water anywhere is now boiling, but the property is displayed whenever any water does boil at sea level. The color of a surface is displayed when light is falling on it and not otherwise. But if color is a property of colored things, they are of course still colored in the dark. This is obviously the ordinary concept of the colors of things, and it is widely held by philosophers and others to be mistaken. This view has even infected some writers of physics textbooks who speak of our color *sensations* and then give an account of light and color that is incompatible with there being any such things as color sensations; they take color, as we all do, to be a real property of things. Physically, surface color is the property of reflecting light of some wavelengths and absorbing that of others. Differences of color are differences of the wavelengths reflected and absorbed—not representations of these differences, but these differences. The results of mixing various pigments are accounted for in the same way. Color-blind people cannot discriminate all the differences that others do. Owing to differences in our visual apparatus, not all colors appear the same to everyone—to appear is to be perceived—but the property that appears is the same property.

A surface that is yellow in daylight is dark red in the light of a black light bulb. Think what Berkeley would have made of that. But it gives no ground for holding that color is not a real property of things. What we have in this case is two related properties. Some of the wavelengths of natural light are not present in black light. Obviously these two properties cannot be displayed at the same time. But many arguments to show the mind-dependence of color demand that if a thing has two colors it must display them both at once. Their authors had assumed that color was not a property, but a type of *quale*. But it would be just as absurd to say that a man does not really play both golf and tennis since he never plays them both at once.

To appear is to be perceived. Colors would not appear if they were not perceived. But what is perceived is a real property, not an appearance. The suggestion that scientific descriptions are or purport to be absolute while macro-observational descriptions are relative corresponds to what was formerly regarded as a difference in the ontological status of the things described and of the properties ascribed to them. But the fact that only some things appear gives no ground for such a distinction. It is only if we hold that what appears is appearances and not real things and that real things cause or are *behind* the appearances, that we get the difference in ontological status. The criterion of independent reality on that view is such that nothing real could conceivably appear or be perceived.

Human perceptual capacities are obviously limited and specialized, like those of other animals, in different ways. They are also capable of diverse development with practice and experience, some of a highly specialized and subtle kind. But it does not follow from this that what we or any other kind of animals perceive is not independently real. Perceptible things are the point of departure for inquiry into what else there is. But it never follows from the existence of something that is imperceptible that what *is* perceptible is mind-dependent.

The fragility of the dualist pillar of the classical doctrine is sufficiently demonstrated by the failure of Descartes, or anyone else, to give any noncircular answer to these questions: Granted that something thinks and perceives, how do we know it is a mind? How *could* we know it is a mind, since we do not know what a mind is? Why should an extended thing not think and perceive? Since people are material beings—ponderable entities—and it is of them that we predicate thought and perception, it is clearly not absurd to say that a material being thinks or perceives. We all know we do. Only if we already think of the material being as a person's body and not a person, and as itself just a machine—and thus beg the question—must we conclude that if something thinks or perceives, it must be something else, viz., an immaterial being.

What Hume says "philosophy teaches" thus consisted of a set of dubious assumptions and dubious arguments based upon them, and skepticism with regard to the senses rested squarely on what "philosophy teaches." The problem of the "external world" was a perennial problem of philosophy whose perennity was assured in the usual way by those who purported to tackle it; to grasp the problem one must already have accepted the assumptions and arguments that would forbid any solution. If these assumptions and arguments had been rejected as they were by unphilosophical people—in much the same way as people reject Zeno's conclusions against motion, though they cannot see the catch—not merely skepticism but most of what was known as epistemology would have gone down the drain. Philosophical argument was therefore conducted in such a way that the bottom did not thus fall out of it, and the mark of a philosophical mind was that it had tacitly undertaken to play the game and see that this did not happen. The case was similar in theology. The initiation of generations to philosophy was an initiation to this game and to the special vocabulary required to play it (ideas, mental events, etc.), and many of the duffers were simply people who, reasonably enough, refused to play.

Of course, nobody really believes a word of it. How could people, when they know better, when even the causal theory of perception depends on some knowledge of their own physiology? One philosopher who recognized this in a backhanded way even in his performance was Hume: Philosophers, he says, "immediately upon leaving their closets, mingle with the rest of mankind in those exploded opinions, that our perceptions are our only objects, and continue identically and uninterruptedly the same in all their interrupted appearances."[6] Within the performance, of course the point cannot be put quite straightforwardly; the admission has to be backhanded. It is not the opinion of mankind that there are such objects as perceptions, far less that they are our only objects, but simply that the principal objects of sight and touch are material things. It is the philosopher's opinion that "what any common man calls a hat or shoe or stone" is a perception, and it is this opinion, if any, that is exploded when he mingles with the rest of mankind, puts his hat or shoes on, kicks a stone, or does anything at all in his closet or out of it. But it is not really *exploded*. The philosopher himself does not really believe it; even the reference to mankind shows as much.

It is a fundamental rule of the game to dissociate perception from action. To find Berkeley or Hume persuasive, one must not think of what it is like—though you know perfectly well what it is like—to clamber over rocks, shovel coal, or fall off a bicycle. The performance requires a contemplative attitude in which you regard what you see before you as if it were a two-dimensional picture of what you see before you. But as a matter of fact from our earliest years we inescapably encounter and mess about with what Ryle called chunky things, being ourselves chunky things. The empiricist notion of the senses and of sense experience entails the denial that these encounters with independent material things are matters of sense experience. Hume actually defines the senses in such a way that they cannot be: as the inlets of impressions, and not the capacity to see, hear, and touch, far less the abilities to look, watch, listen, grasp, and manipulate. Sense experience, in his doctrine, is clearly not sense experience as we have it. Sense experience as it actually is, is therefore made to masquerade as "the opinion of mankind," "the popular system," and in later doctrines, common sense beliefs, common sense realism, direct realism, or the common sense theory. These very expressions all imply that sense experience is something else on which our actual experience, the so-called theory, is founded. In Ayer's version, it is the content of sense experience or statements about this content that provides evidence for statements about material objects, these statements being, or expressing, perceptual judgments. The judgment is made on the basis of the content. But if there is no such thing as the content, there can be no such thing as the judgment, either in our case or in the case of a dumb animal running to retrieve a ball.

The distinction between sense experience and perceptual judgment in some versions recalls Kant rather than Hume, but in the older tradition it is meant to be a factual distinction that does not depend on how the experiences are described or the judgments expressed. Strawson sums up the difference between his own and Ayer's positions thus: "Whereas Ayer says we take a step beyond our sensible experience in making our perceptual judgments, I say rather that we take a step back (in general) from our perceptual judgments in framing accounts of our sensible experience; for we have (in general) to include a reference to the former in framing a veridical description of the latter."[7] Strawson's point is like the one Quine makes when he says that there is no "conceptual subbasement of language." But the fact that we must use material-thing terms to make ourselves intelligible does not result simply from the fact that such terms happen to be fundamental in our language. It is because material things are themselves objects of sense experience, that is, of visual and tactual perception and of practical experience, and because we are ourselves material beings with a back, front, and sides, a top end and a bottom end, that such terms are fundamental in our language.

According to Strawson, to frame an account of a visual experience as distinct from the things we see, we have to preface the description of what we see with the words, "My visual experience is such as it would have been natural to describe in these terms . . ." or to use some similar device.[8] But though Strawson ostensibly accepts the same distinction as Ayer between the contents and the judgment, the classic doctrine in his account really dissolves into the commonplace. He has in effect stopped playing the game. His formula really amounts to no more than saying that what we see looks like what we would naturally say we saw—and perhaps be wrong. But to describe anything as like something, we must know what it is like is like; to say something is like, or looks like a horse, we must know what a horse is like. We are reduced to saying what things look like when they are too far off or it is too dark for us to make out what they are—or when our eyesight is poor or we have lost our glasses. But in cases where we have a good view of them, and still more when we have them in our grasp, this would amount to saying they were just like what they plainly were. If you were riding a horse and anxiously trying to stay on, it would be ludicrous to say your experience was just like that of riding a horse and anxiously trying to stay on.

In his reply to Strawson, Ayer says that if anyone were convinced by Berkeley that what we call physical objects do not exist unperceived, it would not follow that his sense experiences were radically different from those of the ordinary man.[9] But to be convinced of anything by Berkeley, one must first be convinced that his analysis of sense experience is true. But if we take sense experience as we have it, it is easy to show that one after another of his descriptions and analyses is false. If they applied to anything, they would apply to sense experience as it putatively was before it was as it is now, and there is no reason to believe that it ever was so. Many people have been persuaded by Berkeley, in the peculiar way in which people are persuaded philosophically but not really, and of course it would not follow from this that their sense experience was different from anyone else's, but only that they were wrong about their sense experience, that they had failed to notice or ignored the many perfectly familiar differences that Berkeley fails to distinguish, and probably that they had brought to their consideration of the subject the same heavy load of prior assumptions as Berkeley.

Ayer's account of "the transformation of our percepts into visuotactual continuants"[10] is not intended, he says, either as a work of fiction or as a contribution to genetic psychology.[11] Following the example of Russell and Carnap, it is meant to draw out the implications of our ordinary perceptual judgments by a process of "fictive construction."[12] The earliest example of such a "fictive construction" is no doubt Hume's account in the *Treatise* of the belief in body. But what is meant by "fictive"? The question to be asked about any such account of the transformation of percepts into chunky things is whether it is supposed to be true. If it is, then it must be a genetic or developmental account, as Hume's appears to be. Ayer's is intended, he says, to be an account of how an observer might arrive at something like "the common sense view of the world." If we have to arrive at any such thing, then either this is how we do it or it is not. Nobody doubts that perceptual and motor skills develop. What is incredible is that this is how they first develop—from phenomenalism to chunky things. Ayer remarks that he would naturally be gratified if psychological evidence supported his account.[13] In other words, he would be pleased if it were true. But if it were true, it would be a true account of infantile development. Most philosophers nowadays shy away from that or disclaim any such intent. But then what are they up to in their quasi-genetic accounts? Quine, in *Word and Object*, purports to tell us how a toddler gets singular terms and their referents sorted out from general terms and mass terms, according to his peculiar grammatical and categorial doctrine, or what I call his metaphysical parsing. Like a true empiricist toddler, this one gapes at the passing show and hears sounds, associating certain sounds with features of the show, but never grabs, falls, bumps, or even toddles.

The observer in Ayer's story is clearly no infant. But neither is he an adult. The only sense I can make of the notion of observation is that it consists of looking at, watching, listening, touching, exploring, scrutinizing, and examining various things to see what they are like and how they behave. When they are within our reach or grasp, we manipulate them in various ways to see how they react. These activities are possible only for a being that acts, a material being with a back, front, and sides for whom things are there to be observed. In the classic empiricist doctrine, the paradigm case of an immediate impression or sense datum apprehended as such was a pain. Colors and sounds, said Hume, were originally like the pain of the cutting steel. And Berkeley begins his analysis of sensible qualities in the *Dialogues* with heat, assimilating an intense heat to a pain, and arguing thence that other degrees of heat are no less immediate sensations. But pains, being themselves feelings or sensations and not objects or properties of objects, cannot be *observed* or examined. They can only be felt. There is no distinction between feeling a pain and the pain one feels. An unfelt pain is no pain at all. (Though they are otherwise unlike bodily sensations, it is worth remarking that after-images cannot be observed or examined either: you have them but you cannot look at them or away from them.) If all the original data were immediate in the sense in which pains are immediate—they are sensations—it is just as inconceivable that any of them should be transformed into things composed of matter like wooden tables and chairs, as it is that pain should be.

Quasi-genetic constructions like Hume's, Ayer's, Quine's, and many others are examples of a well-known type of so-called theory. They are myths. Though myths were recognized as myths in something like the familiar sense from ancient times through the contrast with *logos* and especially by Plato, they have continued to play a fundamental and highly ambiguous role in many metaphysical doctrines. One example is the so-called theory of the original social contract or compact. In its seventeenth century versions it is ostensibly genetic or historical. But we are told it is not really so or not really meant to be. Another is of course the doctrine of the Fall and Original Sin. As it was formerly understood, and still is by fundamentalists, Original Sin is inherited by us all in virtue of our descent from Adam. Others hold that it must not be understood literally, but as having the kind of truth that a myth has. But what kind of truth is that? It is no good saying it is metaphorically true. Plato's myth of the cave is an expression of part of his doctrine in the form of an allegory or extended metaphor. But genetic myths are not allegories; they are fictitious accounts of how things came to be as they are, or as they are supposed to be. Whereas in religion genetic myth comes first and doctrine later, in secular metaphysics it is doctrine first and myth later. The ambiguous status of such myths in metaphysics merely reflects the ambivalence of metaphysical faith: not even their authors really believe them. For that, they would have to be straight factual theories, and as such there is nothing to support them.

NOTES

1. Descartes, *Oeuvres Philosophiques*. Tome II, p. 431. "qu'il y avait des choses hors de moi, d'où procédaient ces idées, et auxquelles elles étaient tout à fait semblables."
2. Ibid., Objections III, 2 and 3, pp. 600-607.
3. *Enquiry*, p. 152.
4. Ibid., p. 153.
5. Ibid., p. 152.
6. *Treatise*, p. 216.

7. P. F. Strawson, "Perception and its Objects," in *Perception and Identity: Essays Presented to A. J. Ayer*, edited by G. F. Macdonald (Ithaca, N.Y.: Cornell University Press, 1979), pp. 45-46.

8. Ibid., p. 43.

9. Ibid., p. 292.

10. Ibid., p. 293.

11. Ibid., p. 42.

12. Ibid., p. 289.

13. Ibid.

2

Stuff, Kinds, and Causality

The problem of stuff posed by Berkeley was not solved by later empiricists. Hume's account of the belief in body, of the transformation of percepts into visuo-tactual continuants (in Ayer's apt phrase), collapses because the bodies would be immaterial bodies. His analysis of causality is intimately connected with this fact, and a whole doctrinal tradition descending from that analysis depends on ignoring what we know of substances, in the ordinary sense of kinds of stuff like coal, wood, or copper, and of their properties—how they act and react under various conditions.

Impressions and ideas are not of course composed of matter. But if, as Hume says, the vulgar take their perceptions to be their only objects, and if what any man calls a hat or shoe or stone is in fact a perception, what is one to make of the belief, not just that they exist unperceived, but that they are composed of stuff—hats of felt or tweed, shoes of leather, stones of stone, and one might add people of flesh, blood, and bone? Hume gives no account, absolutely none, of how any kind of stuff ever gets into the picture. If we feigned the continuous existence of the perception that we take to be a hat, it would not be composed of felt or some other matter, unless we also feigned the felt or other matter. The idea of matter depends in Hume's view on that of solidity or impenetrability, which for him is the impossibility of the annihilation of one body by another. This idea is not a copy of any impression. "Our modern philosophy, therefore," he concludes, "leaves us no just or satisfactory idea of solidity; nor consequently of matter."[1]

It is because of the trouble about stuff that the famous account of causality is so strange. The commonest way to speak of causation is to use transitive action verbs. One of the types of causal relation obtaining between Mohammed Ali and some other boxers was that he knocked them down and, in some cases, out. He was the cause of their downfall. In Hume's account the relation is not between things or people but between events, and the reason for this is that, in Hume's account, there is in effect no stuff. Questions about the nature of physical interactions are questions of mechanics and matter theory. But the occurrence of many interactions is no less a basic fact of experience and observation than the existence of things composed of stuff. The literature on causality inspired by Hume has been little concerned with actions, reactions, and interactions or with their results, but instead with the concepts of cause and effect understood as distinct events and with the "nature" of the causal relation as a relation between distinct events. These concepts are extremely difficult to apply to many clear and obvious cases of action and reaction. When the wind fills a sail, there is no distinguishable event before the filling of the sail and the movement of the boat, and none while the sail remains filled and the boat is moving. But of course the wind moves the boat—it is not the movement of the boat or the filling of the sail that makes the wind blow. The same goes for the heating of water over a fire, the milling of flour, the sawing of wood, the boiling of potatoes, the distillation of alcohol, the digestion of nutrients, or the action of enzymes on organic substances. Which and how many events would one pick out? Whichever they were, the action of one thing on another—of the millstones on the corn or of the boiling water on the potatoes—would have been conjured away, just as matter is conjured away in Berkeley's analysis of an apple as a congeries of qualities, and only succession would remain. In the case of a footballer kicking a ball, the Humean analysis requires that the swing of the boot count as one event and the flight of the ball as another, but what does not count is the kick—the action of boot on ball. As in Cartesian physics, there is only figure and motion. Since there is no action, there can be no forces. Of course we know the action of anything on anything solely by experience and inference based upon it. It did not take Hume to discover that. What is remarkable in his account is that there is *no* action of anything on anything.

Hume's problem of induction cannot really be understood in any but his own strictest terms: successions are successions of impressions, and the problem is how we can know that past regularities will obtain in the future or that there will be any future. The causal relation depends upon custom or natural induction; what is present to the senses is never anything but impressions, any belief or reasoning about what is not present to the senses is possible only by some causal relation to what is present, and the belief in body itself depends upon induction and causality. The problem of skepticism with regard to the senses and the problem of induction are thus cognate problems with a single source. But if material objects are basic objects of experience and if interactions are in many cases no less perceptible than the things that interact, neither our knowledge of the material things nor our knowledge of their interactions depend upon induction. Of course it depends on experience, but it is experience of the things themselves and of their interactions. If the presuppositions of Hume's problem thus vanish, is there still a problem of induction?

It is possible to speak of things in the usual way, as Hume does— one cannot give concrete examples otherwise—and just assume that the problem remains. One of his examples is the belief that bread will continue to nourish us. But the example can be spelt out only on his assumptions. He is thinking with the learned. First let us speak and think with the vulgar. To identify a piece of stuff as bread is to assume that it has some properties, the principal ones being that it is edible and that it is nourishing. Anything that did not have these properties would not be bread or at least not fresh bread, but at best something that looked or felt to the touch very like bread in one or other of its varieties. To recover Hume's problem, we must think with the learned and go back to what, as he takes it, we really perceive when we perceive a piece of bread—not a piece of stuff but a set of visual qualities and tactual qualities and doubtless gustatory and olfactory qualities that have become associated by custom or habit in such a way that on the occurrence of some we expect the others. The joint set of these qualities are in turn associated with various sensations—corresponding to the activity of chewing and swallowing bread—and with various subsequent phenomena that cannot be detailed in phenomenalist terms at all. So the Humean question is not really whether bread will continue to nourish us— bread being a kind of stuff—but whether such a set of visual and tactual qualities will be followed by the sensations with which it has come to be associated. On this account, the bread, so far as perception goes, is still immaterial bread and no actions or reactions such as occur when one chews up bread and swallows it are matters of sensible experience. *A fortiori*, there are no actual perceptible *properties*. (To ascribe a property to anything is to say that it does or will act or react in certain ways under certain conditions, but not of course that it is at any particular time acting or reacting in any of these ways.) The so-called visible qualities are not really *qualities*: they are what Ayer, Goodman, and others call *qualia*, for they are not as they are given to perception qualities of *anything* or *any stuff*. On these assumptions, the problems of induction and of scepticism with regard to the senses arise and cannot be dispelled.

But if we know by experience that there are material things and stuffs and various types of interaction, the problem, if there is one, reduces to the question of how we know there are kinds of things and kinds of stuff. As we noted in the case of bread, to identify anything as a piece of a certain kind of stuff is to assume that it has certain properties. Let us dramatize this point about properties. Imagine that a child throws you a rubber balloon and, playfully, instead of catching it, you receive it in the face. Surprise! Your nose is broken, blood flows, and you lose your front teeth. Or imagine that some villain bashes you on the head with a baseball bat. Surprise again! It bounces off like a child's balloon without leaving a trace. How could anything so light and elastic as a child's balloon break a nose made of rigid bone and cartilage? How could a baseball bat, very hard and heavy, fail to make any impression on a human head, a fragile thing in comparison? To use these terms—light, elastic, rigid, hard, heavy, fragile—is to say or imply that what we have imagined is impossible, that such things could not happen if the objects in question were indeed a child's balloon and a human face in the first case, and a baseball bat and a human cranium in the second. If your nose were broken on contact with a balloon, it could not be the balloon that broke it, and if there was nothing else to break it, it would have had to undergo some altogether unprecedented internal change.

Of course we can easily imagine one thing changing into another kind of thing: Lot's wife into a pillar of salt, Daphne into a laurel bush, or a prince into a toad at a touch of the wicked fairy's wand.

But if we say such things are impossible, it is because these are kinds of things or beings with properties. To ascribe properties to anything is to say how it will act or react and also how it will not act or react under various conditions. The relevant properties of a normal human nose are rigid but relatively brittle bone and flexible but quite tough cartilage. Such a nose *cannot* be broken by a casual encounter with a child's balloon.

Now it is quite possible to establish the properties of one thing or one piece of stuff. Inference comes into the picture, not prior to any such discovery, but subsequently when we infer from the fact that another thing has some of these properties that it has the others as well. If we can determine the properties in one case we can determine them in another and verify the inference. In practice of course we assume a great deal and do not bother to verify that things are of the kinds we take them for by habit. But habit is not fundamental—such assumptions can be verified or falsified, for they do not require any invalid jump from some cases to all. There is no presupposition here at this humble prescientific level, where our only problem is not to mistake one kind of thing for another as we easily can, of any such principle as the universal regularity of nature, or of the principle that the future will be like the past. These are, in any case, different principles. The future in many respects will not be like the past: it will be like it only in so far as there are the same kinds of things (having the same properties) as there were in the past. If it is true that even the chemical elements have evolved locally in the universe, even these natural kinds did not always exist, and the past was thus unlike the present—and so may the future be for all we know. The universal regularity of nature used to be understood as the indifference of natural laws to mere space and time. Since space and time, it turns out, are not mere, it has now to be understood as the principle that there are fundamental laws of the universe consistent with the laws that obtain locally—in our region of space-time, for example, the laws of chemistry and biology. These laws are universal only in the trivial sense that they apply to everything of the kinds to which they apply.

One way of contesting the view that there is no problem of induction but only the familiar practical problem of not mistaking one kind of thing for another (as we sometimes do) is to maintain that we cannot establish the properties of one thing—nor, therefore, that anything is any kind of thing—without making assumptions that cannot be empirically verified or justified, just as inductive inference cannot be in the classic doctrine. This would not bring back the problem of induction but it would raise a problem very like it.

Suppose we take a piece of wire, not knowing what metal or alloy it is made of, and bend it. We now know we bent it and that it is bent. Does it follow from this directly, without any nonempirical assumptions, that it is flexible? To say it is flexible usually implies that it would have bent if we had tried to bend it earlier and that it will bend again if we try to bend it again. In the case of wire, we assume this without knowing what kind of wire it is, because we have no experience of wire that bends at one time and will not bend two minutes later under ordinary household conditions, not because we jump to the invalid conclusion that all wire that can be bent at one time can be bent again two minutes later. But suppose our wire will not bend two minutes later; at first it is unyielding and then, with increased pressure, it suddenly breaks. We know what happened on these two occasions, not what would have happened or will happen on any other occasion. When we bent it, it was flexible, and when we broke it, it was brittle. Is that all? No, we also know that, being flexible, it can become brittle within two minutes. Many properties are of short duration. Thus the viscosity of cement or grout, which is immediately evident from its behavior when it is scooped up, poured, or slapped down, is lost as it hardens, and this change of property is a property essential to the purposes for which it is used. Any perceptible stuff has perceptible properties whether they last for a long time or a short time. But does any change of property manifest a property? We know why the wire bent when it was flexible—we bent it—and we know why it broke when it was brittle—we broke it. But we do not know why, being flexible, it became brittle. To take this change also as the manifestation of a property is to assume that any change that occurs in it consists of some reaction or set of reactions.

Does this need justification? The classic empiricist version of the causal principle, "Every event has a cause," implies that every change is an event and that its cause is some distinct event. But any action or reaction is itself a change and what we actually assume is that any change is a reaction (or set of reactions), whether or not we know what it is, and that the state of any substance when it ceases is the result. The principle is not that every change has a cause, interpreted in the *classic* way, but that causation—action and reaction—is what change consists of. We may not infer from the fact that some changes do consist of this that all do. We know, however, that some do. But those who believe in miracles claim that some do not, that miracles are possible. What makes legendary transformation miracles miracles is that the subject—Lot's wife, Daphne, or the water at the wedding in Cana of Galilee—has no natural physical properties such that the transformation could occur. Hence there is no action or reaction but just a great and astounding change. Miracles would not be miracles if they were not physically impossible. The type of possibility claimed for them must be metaphysical: what is physically impossible may be metaphysically possible just as it may be logically possible.

In such stories, what is changed into what depends in no way on the physical properties of either thing. On the contrary, these render the miracle physically impossible. For like reasons, when the performance of miracles is ascribed to supernatural beings or to Jesus, there not only is not, but cannot be, any question of how they did it, as there always is when the performances are those of magicians like Houdini. Any such question implies that the performance is *not* miraculous. The notion of such an immaterial "action" is, however, familiar to all philosophers. It is the one we find ascribed to the human mind or will by Berkeley, Hume, and many others. The difference from the miraculous actions of supernatural beings is just that our minds or wills do their thing—psychokinesis—quite regularly and as a matter of course. It is not that there is no way of *knowing* how the mind does it: the question of how the mind does it is meaningless. A miracle therefore has to be redefined by Hume as what is contrary to the best established regularities. There is no such thing as physical impossibility in his terms. Inductive evidence, however, the only evidence we have, is always overwhelmingly against the truth of any report of a miracle. But in fact when anyone claims that miracles are impossible, he at least means physically impossible whether or not he assumes that what is not physically possible is not possible at all. Those who believe in miracles cannot consistently hold that no change occurs that does not consist of physical reactions, manifestations of the properties of the things in question. But since this notion of what a change consists of is the only one we have, since we have it by experience, and since it requires no extra-empirical assumptions, if anyone wishes by his own agency to prevent, control, or bring about any kind of change, his only recourse is to find out what acts on or interacts with what; or, in practical terms, what to do with what and to what, to get the desired result. The problem of whether, having succeeded once, he can do it again is just that of finding the same kinds of thing and of doing what he did the first time, not that of knowing whether he will obtain the same result if he does.

Though we can indeed discover the properties of one thing and find others of the same kind and thence proceed to distinguish as many kinds and subkinds as occasion demands, original discovery is not the only or even the principal way in which we learn about kinds of things and their properties. But it is fundamental to all the other ways that we have this way and can use it in practice.

NOTE

1. *Treatise*, p. 229.

3

Animals and Their Bodies

Many philosophers assume, since the notion of a soul or mind is
quite ancient and familiar to everyone and since many people profess a belief in the soul or mind, that the dualist concept of a human
being as the union of two things is the popular one and that most
people are in fact mind-body dualists. But it is important as always
to distinguish professions of metaphysical belief from beliefs which
are not professed but simply manifested in common speech and action.
It is clear that in ancient as in modern times, people have in all
practical contexts always ascribed actions, thoughts, and feelings to
people, the very same beings to which they ascribe physical characteristics, and not to immaterial beings such as souls would be. Those
who believe in the soul have continually spoken and acted in practical contexts as if they did not. The reason why they have done
so is that the only identifiable things to which actions, thoughts, and
feelings can be ascribed are these visible, tangible beings. What is
called animism need not be the belief that many kinds of things are
inhabited by souls or, as Thales is supposed to have said, that all
things are full of gods, but just the belief that many things besides
people and animals have emotions, likes, and dislikes, and should
be treated accordingly. Since a human being or an animal is a material
being, it is not surprising that there appears to be no word for the
human body in Homer—*soma* seems to mean a corpse and *demas*
the form or figure of a human being. Since any part of a human
body is a part of a human being, the notion of the human body,
unlike that of arms, legs, and other parts of a human being, is for

all practical purposes dispensable. But it is required of course for the doctrine of body and soul.

Physicalism is largely programmatic: it is generally admitted by physicalists that we have to dodge along for countless purposes with the Old Adam's mentalistic and indeed supernaturalist language till we get something better. The central thesis, however, is essentially that a human being is an organism and the organism in our case is a human body—a living and not a dead one of course. What this boils down to is that a human being and his body, or any animal and its body, are identical. My first purpose is to show that this thesis is false for the same reason that dualism is false, and that the reason lies in the concept of a human body—or any animal's body. Both types of doctrine take it that in the case of human beings, the material entity is certainly the human body. And both doctrines take it that the denial of the identity of a human being and his body entails that there is something immaterial over and above this material entity. Even Strawson, who rejects both these doctrines, shares this concept of the human body, and the difficulty in his analysis of the concept of a person lies there.

Physicalists usually employ the expressions "mental event" and "mental state," borrowed from earlier philosophical doctrines, to cover sensations, perceptions, thoughts, emotions, and intentions, and they take it that these terms, as they are commonly used and understood, are what they call mentalistic terms. Since the only material entity is by common accord the body, either mental events are events in a mind and mental states are states of a mind or they are just immaterial phenomena not predicated of anything, and it is this doctrine that physicalists reject. These are of course doctrinal terms. In the sense in which "mental state" is commonly used to cover such things as melancholy or elation, a mental state or a state of mind is not a state of a mind but a state of a human being or person— thus a person is in a certain state of mind. A mental state is thus a state of a material entity or being, since a human being or any other animal is such a being. These are just one class of a very large class of terms that Strawson calls P-predicates, "P" standing for "person."[1] (Strawson uses "predicate" to mean the attribute and not the term or expression by which it is ascribed to or predicated of a subject. I use it to mean the term or expression.) P-predicates apply distinctively to people but not to their bodies. Since many of them

apply to other animals as well as to us, and some predicates apply
only to other animals but not to their bodies, I take P-predicates
to be a subclass of A-predicates ("A" for "animal"). Thus it is a
dog and not a dog's body that loves to run and catch a ball in the
air or to gnaw a bone, that jumps up to lick his master's face, or
that keeps at a safe distance from the cat. But the dog's body no
less than the dog weighs 30 pounds or is covered with hair. "Weighs
30 pounds" and "is covered with hair" can be applied to the animal's
body as well as the animal, and these are what Strawson calls "M-
predicates"—"M" for "material." Most A- and P-predicates are action or activity predicates and of course presuppose physical characteristics. If A- or P-predicates apply to anything, M-predicates must
apply to the very same thing.

According to the common concept of a human being or of a
dog, a chimpanzee, an elephant, and many other animals, all these
animals have bodies. But plants, though they have parts that are
the obvious analogue of animal organs, do not have bodies. Nor,
so far as common discourse goes, do fleas, ticks, nits, lice, or
cockroaches, though they all have quite distinct organs and are certainly all animals. (The body of a bee is just the part of the bee
distinct from the wings, head, legs, and tail.) That an animal has
a body implies that it is not the same thing as its body. But if an
animal is itself a material entity or body, as it obviously is, how
can it be said to have a body? It can only be said to have a body
if the sense of "body" is different from the sense in which it is a
body. Now a whole can of course have distinct parts, and the dualist doctrine is that a human being has two main parts, one material—
his body—and the other immaterial—his mind. His body is a body
in the only sense of "body"—a compact thing composed of matter.
It follows from this that a human being is not a body: the whole
is not one of its parts and it is just as wrong to say a human being
is a body as it is to say he is a leg (a part of one of the two main
parts, the body). Though dualists have rarely observed this, the same
would go for a dog and its body, for if a dog has a body it is in
exactly the sense in which a human being does. Thus the dualist
doctrine is in flat conflict with what everyone knows, that a human
being, like a dog, is a visible, tangible, ponderable entity and obviously
in that sense a body, a compact thing composed of matter. And
it need hardly be said that those who profess a dualist doctrine

constantly talk and act as if it were not true. The sense of "body" in which a person or animal has a body is not the sense in which he is one. On one point, however, dualists are right, at least implicitly: the sense in which a human being or animal *has* a body is the same sense as that in which he *has* arms, legs, a heart, and other organs. But they conclude from this that just as these are parts, so the whole body is a part made up of all these parts, and that a human being has another part, the immaterial one.

What then is the concept of the body? There are two principal contexts in which we speak of people's bodies or of *the* body, meaning the human body: aesthetic contexts and physiological or medical contexts. In aesthetic contexts, the usual expression for the whole body is "the human figure" or "the human form" and this seems to be the sense also of the Greek *demas*. What is meant by "a beautiful body" or "an ungainly body" does not usually include the head or face. A person may have a beautiful body but a plain face, and "body" sometimes means only the trunk or torso. But apart from this type of context, broadly speaking aesthetic, what people mean by "the body" is the whole system of organs, their functions in the system, and the mechanisms of these functions, in other words, all the works, on which of course all the actions and activities of the animal depend. I use the term "works" in the sense in which we speak of the works of a watch. But whereas the works of a watch do not include the case or the face of the watch, the works of a human being do include the skin and external organs as well as the internal ones. It is not, however, the person's works that play tennis, but the person. It is not the dog's works that chase a rabbit, but the dog. And the sense of "has" in which a person or a dog has a body is the same as the sense in which he, she, or it has legs, a brain, a digestive system, ductless glands, and so on, for the body is just that, the whole works.

The dead body of an animal and the dead animal are the same thing, and when people speak of a human body or a dog's body they often mean a corpse or carcass. And whether a person gives instructions where to bury him when he is dead or where to bury his body, what is buried will obviously be one and the same thing.

In *Individuals*, Strawson is first concerned to show that our basic particulars or primary objects of reference are and must be material things or bodies in the sense of "material things," more or less compact things composed of stuff. But in the subsequent chapter on persons, he says, "that which one calls one's body is, at least, a body, a material thing. It can be picked out from others, identified by ordinary physical criteria, and described in ordinary physical terms."[2] If what he says were so, the concept of that kind of body—a human body—would be on a par with concepts of other kinds of body or material things such as rocks, tables, houses, cars, trees, or any other basic particular. But this cannot be so if a person is a body or material thing. That a person is a body is evident from the fact that M-predicates apply to him or her, but that he is not identical with his body is evident from the fact that P-predicates apply to *him* but not to *it*. If they are both bodies in the same sense of "body," they are not the same body but different ones, and one should be able to weigh or otherwise measure them one against the other. But in fact, as we all know, all the predicates of a human body apply exactly to the human being. One's own body or anyone's body is, of course, a human body. A *human* body can be picked out from others, identified by ordinary physical criteria, and described in ordinary physical terms, only if we can identify human beings. We can identify a human being and pick him out from others. We do not *need* to pick out his body and in fact there is nothing distinct from *him* to pick out: his body is wherever he is.

Now Strawson's principal thesis is that the concept of a person is primitive. What he means by this may be understood in part by his statement that it is "not to be analyzed as that of an animated body or of an embodied *anima*"[3]—for in that case the concepts of a human body and a human *anima* or soul would be primitive— and in part by his statement that the concept of an individual consciousness is "logically secondary" or, in other words, derivative from that of the person whose consciousness it is.[4] But Strawson never claims that the concept of a human *body* is derivative. The reason is clear: he takes the body to be itself a material thing of a certain kind, identifiable—like any other material thing—by the criteria for that kind, and not derived from the concept of a person as is that of an individual consciousness or mind. But in fact it is derivative or logically secondary. Not only that, but we can very well do without it, since whatever we want to say about *it* can equally be said of the human being or animal.

Strawson's thesis that the concept of a person is primitive is not a claim about the doctrines that people hold or the various concepts that figure in these doctrines but about the concept that is manifested in their words and deeds when they are not professing any doctrine at all. It is obvious from the most ancient literatures that people have always had this concept, and that P- and M-predicates have always been applied to human beings. Naturally, M-predicates are far less common than P-predicates, but if they did not also apply there would of course be no actions. But doubtless most people, if asked whether their bodies were material things in Strawson's sense, would answer impromptu that *of course* they are. They are certainly not immaterial things, are they? And it is doubtless because Strawson asked himself that question that he gives the obvious answer and asserts quite casually that what one calls one's body is at least a body, a material thing. If, however, the concept of a person is the one that is constantly manifested in talk and action, this is not what people really believe and in fact know. They know that human beings, the referents of personal pronouns and proper names, are material, ponderable entities as are other animals, but that they are not identical with their bodies— they *have* bodies. If these bodies were also material, ponderable entities, they would be different ones. But nobody believes there are two material entities: the one he *is* and the one he *has*. It must be remembered, however, that no metaphysical doctrine is so deep-rooted, widespread, and truly popular as that of the two things, body and mind (or soul), and according to this doctrine the body is of course the material thing. To question people about their beliefs in this matter is to invite an exposition of their preferred doctrine. The doctrinal focus of interest was always upon the invisible, intangible, immaterial, and therefore problematic and mysterious thing, which might survive death, and not upon the other thing, the obvious one. Hence, even those who denied the existence of the soul, or denied that it was an entity or substance, took the body for granted and assumed that it at any rate was an entity or substance, a material one, just as dualists from Plato to Descartes and later always have.

It follows from the fact that a human being, the referent of a proper name and of personal pronouns, is a material entity like any other animal, that if anything can be disembodied (whatever that means) it is not a human being. I have so far used "human being" often where Strawson uses "person" since it makes no difference to the essential points at issue. But if the concept of a person is taken to be a moral, legal, or, as Locke has it, a forensic concept, one may of course hold that not all human beings are persons and that some nonhuman beings, if there are such in other galaxies or elsewhere in this, might qualify as persons. But this moral concept of a person is the concept of some kind of being who is a person. What I mean is that "person" does not then signify a kind of being as "human being," "cat" and "dog" do, or as a term signifying some kind of being or creature from outer space would. In this respect, it would be like "musical genius" or "physicist." Just as there might conceivably be nonhuman persons, so there might conceivably be nonhuman musical geniuses or physicists. It follows that the identity of a person, like that of a physicist or a musical genius, is dependent on that of the being who is a person. A being might, and according to some concepts of a person does, have to become a person, but for as long as he was a person, the same person would be the same being, e.g., the same human being.

Locke, in his account of personal identity, fails to grasp this point. Part of the time, he clearly assumes that "person" itself signifies a kind of being, not necessarily a human being, so that the same person could conceivably at different times be different human beings or even different kinds of animal, or that he could be incarnated in different beings at different times. On this tack, there is no way of distinguishing a person from a soul or mind, the Cartesian—no less than Lockean—something-we-know-not-what that thinks and, especially, remembers. But Locke also maintains that consciousness makes or constitutes the person.[5] By "consciousness" he means recall—consciousness of the past—and especially the capacity to recall having done, felt, and thought various things, that is to say, the capacity to be conscious of being the very one who did, felt, and thought these things. Thus, without consciousness of identity, there is no personal identity. But since the episodes recalled are discontinuous, so must be the person. The one who did certain things that he now recalls may be the same *man* who did other things that he does not now recall, but he is not the same *person*. If he was a person when he did the things he does not now recall doing, he was a different person. But if he then recalled doing things that he still recalls doing, the person who did these things is identical with each of two persons who are not themselves identical, which is absurd.

Since the identity of a person in the forensic sense is dependent upon that of a being of some kind, and so far as we are concerned on that of a human being, and a human being cannot be disembodied, neither can a person be disembodied. An immaterial mind or soul is not inconceivable in the usual sense of being a flagrant impossibility. The problem is that we do not conceive it, that we have no concept of it, that it is something-we-know-not-what, a Lockean substance. We do have the terms "mind," "soul," and "spirit," and these have many idiomatic and perfectly intelligible uses. It is when they purport to signify a kind of entity that the concept is lacking. But countless people have supposed and do suppose that they know what is meant by these terms and that they do at least conceive the kind of thing even if they deny that there is any such thing. If Descartes did not suppose that he conceived such a thing, his proof of its real existence (as an entity or substance distinct from the body) would not merely be invalid but could not even be attempted. We do understand texts in which it is the main topic just as we understand texts in which God is the main topic. But that does not entail that we have a concept of it. We do have the concept of a being or entity distinct from that of a property or relation or activity—beings or entities, as in Aristotle, are one category of thing in the noncategorial sense of "things," and men and horses are cases in point, kinds of beings. But whereas we do have concepts of *these* kinds of beings, we have no concept of the kind of being that "soul" or "mind" is supposed to mean. The traditional reproach to those who say what I am saying is that they are illegitimately demanding that a being must be a material being whereas, of course, the beings in question are immaterial. This does not meet the point. The point is that men and horses are not something-we-know-not-what—they are not Lockean substances—but minds or souls are. If we speak of we-know-not-what, we do not know what we are talking about, not in the usual sense that we are saying preposterous things about something, but in the unusual sense that we do not know what we are saying them about. This is very common in metaphysical writings. I take an example from Strawson, which is of special interest since it runs directly counter to the principal points in his analysis of the concept of a person.

Strawson maintains that "from within our actual conceptual scheme, each of us can quite intelligibly conceive of his or her individual survival of bodily death. The effort of imagination is not even great."[6] The question is: What is it that each of us can conceive as surviving bodily death? It cannot be the human being—the human being would be dead—nor can it therefore be the person. But he or she who is alleged to be able to conceive his or her individual survival is a human being or person. Only if one assumes that he or she is not a human being but something else, can the one who conceives his or her own survival be the one who is conceived as surviving. But the something else is, as always, something-we-know-not-what: we have no concept of it and in the sense explained before, we do not know what we are talking about. Before we examine the rest of this passage on disembodiment, let us look at another passage where, again, something-we-know-not-what makes its spectral appearance. What this passage shows is how the pseudo-concept of disembodiment arises.

Strawson considers what he calls "the unique role each person's body plays in his experience."[7] To illustrate this role, he mentions various obvious facts: one sees only when the eyelids are open and various other physiological conditions are fulfilled; one's seeing something depends on the orientation of the eyes, head, and body, and where one sees from depends on where the body and head are located. Strawson then describes the imaginary case of a subject S, who has—or whose seeing is dependent upon—three different bodies, A, B, and C. S sees from where body C is, when A's eyes are open, in a direction determined by the head and eyeballs of B. In this case, clearly S is not located at all, not facing in any direction, since S is not itself a body. And in what Strawson takes to be the actual case, where S has only one body, this is no less so. So what is S? Not the human being or animal, nor therefore the person, but something-we-know-not-what. We have no concept of S. But if we take the body to be the material entity, since we are not identical with the bodies we have, and if all these facts are just facts about it, we ourselves become the mysterious S, something-we-know-not-what. But these are all facts about us. The head, eyes, and other parts of the body are parts of us. What we can see depends on which way we are facing, where we are located, and what we are looking at. If one asks what role we play in our own experience, the only answer is the trivial one that we look at things and touch and manipulate them, we move about, and so on. There is a similarly obvious answer to the question about what role our hands play—

we grasp and touch things with them. Beyond that, to ask what role any of our organs plays can only be answered by an account of how that organ works.

The dependence of one's experience on facts about a body, says Strawson, "provides a good reason why a subject of experience should have a very special regard for just one body . . . why, granted that I am going to speak of one body as mine, I should speak of this body as mine. But they do not explain why I should have the concept of myself at all, why I should ascribe my thoughts and experiences to *anything* . . ."[8] They do not explain why the experiences and corporeal characteristics should be ascribed to the very same thing. This problem, to which there is no solution, arises from regarding the body as the material entity. If it is, "I" does not refer to that material entity, and since there are not two material entities, it does not refer to any material entity. "I" can only refer to something-we-know-not-what.

Pursuing his claim that we can easily conceive or imagine our survival of bodily death, Strawson says:

> One has simply to think of oneself as having thoughts and memories as at present, visual and auditory experiences largely as at present . . . whilst (*a*) having no perceptions of a body related to one's experience as one's own body is, and (*b*) having no power of initiating changes in the physical condition of the world, such as one at present does with one's hands, shoulders, feet, and vocal chords. Condition (*a*) must be expanded by adding that no one else exhibits reactions indicating that he perceives a body at the point which one's body would be occupying if one were seeing and hearing in the embodied state.[9]

To make my point, it suffices to ask what one would be. One would certainly not be Strawson or Cowley or anyone else. But it turns out that what one imagines is something that countless people have imagined—what it would be like to be invisible, like the man in the movie. Of course, the invisible man has a body, but it is an invisible body. Is there any difference from what Strawson asks us to imagine? If one had auditory and visual experiences largely as at present, one would hear sounds from the right or left, from behind or from in front, above or below. One would see things in the direction in which one was looking but not in the opposite direction, just as one would if one had a body, from just where one's eyes would be if one had eyes, and things would appear in various perspectives near and far, upside down or right side up, according to the orientation one would have if one had a body. Could one turn round or take a closer look at something? Could one push things from where one's hands would be or grasp them, as one would if one had hands? To stop short of this is quite arbitrary. Strawson agrees that we can imagine his condition (*b*) not being fulfilled, but he says, "This would be a rather vulgar fancy, in the class of table-tapping spirits with familiar voices."[10] His unwillingness to go the whole hog in his imaginings rests on the classic empiricist dissociation of perception from action and especially of seeing from looking and watching and moving about to get the best view. So what we imagine is really just being invisible or, if you like, having an invisible body. Imagine reaching for something and grasping it but seeing no arm or hand there. But what we cannot imagine is looking and seeing something in no direction, with no behind or before, no left or right. And this shows that what we are imagining is not having no body, but just being invisible. A sound could not come from behind if we had no behind.

Strawson does attempt an answer to the question what one would be in the disembodied state. His answer is that one would be a former person, the individual consciousness of a person persisting after the body died.[11] But this is another pseudo-concept, no less than that of the pure transcendental consciousness in idealist phenomenology. "To be conscious" has several senses, but in every sense consciousness is a state, not an act or activity or property and certainly no kind of entity or being. There are conscious acts but not acts of consciousness, conscious intentions but not intentions of consciousness, and so-called states of consciousness are just conscious states of a person, not states of a consciousness. Seeing is, if you like, a type of consciousness, the visual consciousness of things. But it is not the consciousness that sees—consciousness is the seeing, not the seer or the seen. Whatever or whoever one would be, surviving bodily death, one would not be a consciousness. Only a conscious being can have any experiences at all. And the only such beings we know of are human beings and other animals, material beings, ponderable entities.

Descartes' physics is hard to reconcile with his notion of an individual, finite material substance. In his doctrine of the plenum, the distinction of matter and space disappears, and a so-called finite substance would be a mode of extension, as it is in Spinoza. But he clearly assumes this notion of the finite material substance in his account of human beings and takes a human body to be a finite extended substance, a concrete entity. Now the Cartesian concept of a finite substance is that it can be and be conceived independently of any other finite substance, whereas properties and relations exist only as properties and relations of substances and cannot be or be conceived apart from them. But by his very own criterion of a substance, a human body or an animal's body is not a substance, for it requires something else to be or be conceived, a human being or an animal. But if the body is taken to be the material entity or complete substance, as it is by Strawson, in spite of his rejection of Cartesian dualism, the kind of thing it is is obviously some kind of natural machine, and one need not know much about the details of the mechanisms to reach this conclusion. This is indeed very like the concept of it that people actually have: it is, as I have put it, all the works. The difference is that, according to the usual concept, it is the works of a human being or animal, this being the concrete entity, whereas according to the Cartesian concept it is itself a concrete, complete entity. In the case of human beings, according to the Cartesian doctrine, there is another entity but in the case of other animals there is no other entity. In his account of all animals but us, Descartes is a physicalist: animals are really what are commonly called their bodies. There is no sense in which an animal has a body. It is a body, and the body it is, is what is mistakenly called *its* body. The usual concept of an animal is thus rejected together with that of a human being. Materialists like LaMettrie and Diderot, who maintained that human beings were animals and denied the existence of Cartesian minds or souls—that counted as materialism in the eighteenth century—had first to maintain that other animals were animals in the usual sense, for according to the Cartesian concept they were not.

The distinction of the animal and its body can be obscured by using the term "organism." If any living thing is an organism, then plants and animals, ourselves included, are organisms. The organism in this case is not the body of the animal but the animal, just as in the case of a plant it is the plant. In this sense of "organism," micro-organisms are bodies in exactly the sense in which we are. But when we speak of the human organism, we mean the human body. The distinction does not disappear if we use the term "organism" sometimes to mean the animal and sometimes its body.

What physicalists really do or try to do is to drop the concept of the animal, just as Descartes did. They do not drop the *term*. But then Berkeley did not drop terms like "gold" or "coal." To make the physicalist thesis substantial, the aim ought to be to get rid of P- and A-predicates, which apply only to the human being or animal and not to its body. But this is not how physicalists conceive physicalism. Their own doctrine is conceived in opposition to other metaphysical doctrines, and it is not their concern to analyze concepts that are no part of any professed doctrine but which are manifest in everyone's speech and practice. They do not waste their time arguing against the doctrine of the second thing of dualism (the mind), but they do take it as their business to dispose of whatever is mental in a sense derived from dualism. They use the standard expressions "mental events," "mental states," "mental entities," and so on. These cannot be used for any purpose but the exposition of doctrines to which they belong, unlike the P-predicates we actually apply, which are all of them predicates of human beings, visible, tangible entities. Though one can only think what might be meant by these terms by thinking of a very small class of P-predicates, doctrinal terms are essential vehicles of delusion in metaphysical performances.

Hume was not a physicalist, but his account of human action in the *Enquiry* requires only two little changes to be cast as a physicalist account.

> It may be said that we are every moment conscious of internal power; while we feel, that, by the simple command of our will, we can move the organs of our body or direct the faculties of our mind. An act of volition produces motion in our limbs, or raises a new idea in our imagination. This influence of the will we know by consciousness. . . . But the means by which this is effected; the energy by which the will performs so extraordinary an operation; of this we are so far from being immediately conscious, that it must for ever escape our most diligent enquiry.[12]
>
> We learn from anatomy, that the immediate object of power in voluntary motion is not the member itself which is moved, but certain muscles, and nerves, and animal spirits, and perhaps, something still more minute and more unknown, through which the motion is suc-

cessively propagated, ere it reach the member itself whose motion is the immediate object of volition.[13]

In this account we are distinct from our bodies, the material things, and we do things that result mysteriously in movements in parts of the body, none of which but the last macro-movement of a limb or the like was ever intended. So we are still intentional agents of a sort, though we do not know how we produce any effect. The first change required to make this a physicalist account is one that Hume already accepted in the *Treatise*. If we ask what a volition is, it is some kind of secondary impression (like a sentiment or feeling), an event caused by antecedent events and associated with an idea. And on this account we do not really do anything, in fact we drop out. Mental events cause physical events in so-called action, and physical events cause mental events in so-called perception. Substitute physical events for the mental events and you have physicalism. Since the gross movements of an animal do indeed have physiological causes, the problem for physicalism is just to dispose of, or account for, the mental events or mental states.

Epiphenomenalism, the view that mental events are inexplicable by-products or accompaniments of some physiological events but without physical effects, is generally agreed to be, like solipsism, not so much a philosophical doctrine as a philosophical disaster. Though T. H. Huxley professed it, it is hard to find anyone who has been content with it, though it is no more preposterous than many more widely held doctrines. It is the desire to avoid it that provides the direct motive for the identity theses of Herbert Feigl, J. J. C. Smart, and some other physicalists. This is made most explicit in Feigl's book *The "Mental" and the "Physical."* Neurophysiological events are to be explained by neurophysiological laws without appeal to any mental event or state. But if so, mental events or states are, as Feigl says, "nomological danglers," not accounted for by these laws, or in other words epiphenomena. But if they can, or could in principle, be correlated with events in the nomological net, and inferred or predicted from these and other nomologically connected events, this being what Feigl calls "extensional equivalence" to their correlates, we can end the scandal of epiphenomenalism by simply taking them to be identical with their correlates. Earlier, cruder versions of this are to be found in Hobbes and Holbach.

The model for a statement that some mental event or state is identical with some brain event or state is provided by such statements as "Lightning is a discharge of electrons," "Water is H_2O," or "Visible light is electromagnetic radiations of between 3500 and 4700 angstroms." It is important to note how they differ from statements like "The Morning Star is the Evening Star" or "Cicero was Tully," where the referent of each term is an identifiable macroobject. Thus one might identify Cicero by one set of descriptions and Tully by another set but not know that Cicero and Tully were not two men but one and the same. In each of the theoretical identity statements what we have in effect is a statement of what something perceptible consists of, with mention of the constituents. Thus we have a perfect paraphrase without loss or gain of sense if we replace "is" by "consists of": "Lightning consists of a discharge of electrons," "Water consists of H_2O molecules." There are similar statements that make no mention of micro-constituents but only of kinds of stuff or ingredients, for example, statements that tell you what bronze or brass, or for that matter cocky-leeky soup or haggis, consist of. These are in effect recipes—they tell you what to do with what to get what.

But the model for mind-brain identity statements is not these but statements like the ones I have mentioned that belong to elaborate bodies of theory of great and systematic explanatory power. Substances are analyzed and tested, and actions and reactions predicted and verified every day in the terms of chemical theory. The reasons for accepting chemical theory are quite independent of anyone's motives. But the mind-brain identity thesis is a doctrine with motives, not a theory with reasons. There is no thought of accounting for any characteristic of any kind of experience, as chemical theory accounts for the macro-properties of different substances (kinds of stuff). The thesis does not even begin with anything obvious like water, light, or lightning, but takes its rise from another metaphysical doctrine. This ancestral doctrine does indeed purport to tell us what experience consists of—raw feels, impressions, sensations, etc. But the identity doctrine does not tell us what raw feels consist of as the model would require, but merely asserts that they are identical with brain events. The idea is solely and unblushingly not to explain or account for anything, but to get the danglers into the nomological net. The trouble, supposing some identity statements of the kind were true, is that it would make no difference to the net or to anything in the net. If the brain events which are mental events had not been mental events, they would still have been the same brain events, and the laws would have been just the same laws. The physical and physiological explanation goes by the brain event, and the animal's behavior would be just the same if no cerebral or neural event were a mental event. The distinction between epiphenomenalism and the identity doctrine is thus a distinction without a difference. The identity would not just be contingent as identity theorists say (in the Humean fashion which makes no distinction between real possibility and epistemic possibility), it would also be inexplicable. From the evolutionary standpoint it would be quite anomalous, since the identity of some brain events with mental events would have no survival value, just as if the mental events were, as in Huxley's doctrine, epiphenomena. It is curious that Huxley did not raise this point.

One reply to this from exponents of the identity thesis is that the objection tacitly assumes that mental events are not really and truly brain events. If they are really and truly identical, to explain and account for the brain event is to explain and account for the mental event. It is just as absurd to think the identity needs to be accounted for as it is to suppose that the identity of Cicero and Tully needs to be accounted for: to account for any fact about Cicero is automatically to account for a fact about Tully. But this reply merely makes plain the motive for the doctrine; it does not answer the objection. *Ex hypothesi*, only *some* brain events are mental events and most of them are not. This is clearly a difference between some and others. But this difference would be unaccounted for in the physiological story of their causation and occurrence. It is only qua brain events that mental events would figure in the account. This difference between the brain events that were mental events and those that were not would make no difference.

The identity thesis has fallen from favor, though nothing, however preposterous, ever simply dies in philosophy. Most physicalists now seem to regard what they call mentalist terms as irremediably mentalist, but accept that we are condemned to use them for want of anything better. Physicalism and behaviorism are as closely related as the doctrines they respectively reject—mentalism, the doctrine that there are mental states and events, and introspectionism, the doctrine of how we know there are. A behaviorist, it may be thought, need not hold that animals and their bodies are identical but simply that only their bodies and bodily movements are observable. Behaviorism is sometimes said to be methodological solipsism. But in this as in other cases, methodology rests on metaphysics, and if they are distinct what is obscure is the method not the metaphysics. A solipsist problem certainly arises from the doctrine that all we can ever observe of so-called animals and human beings is their bodies and bodily movements. It also follows from this doctrine that the ordinary terms in which we describe people's behavior and ask questions and receive answers concerning it must be theoretical terms signifying things that we cannot in principle ever observe or know by acquaintance.

For those physicalists who, like Quine, take a language to be a conceptual system or theory and for whom nothing can be, so to speak, *known* outside a theoretical framework, to find a satisfactory set of terms with which to replace the usual "mentalist" ones is the same thing as finding a better theory. Where genuine theories are concerned, finding suitable terms is hardly a problem at all. That is because genuine theories are advanced in answer to substantial questions or as solutions to substantial problems. The trouble is not that physicalism is programmatic, but that it is not clear what the program is. A genuine program would be a set of problems it proposed to tackle. But is physicalism itself not a theory? Only in the linguistic transcendentalist sense of "theory," not in the sense in which the theory of natural selection and the theory of atomic weights of the elements are theories. It is a metaphysical doctrine, just as dualism is. Linguistic transcendentalism does not fit theories in the ordinary sense; it only fits metaphysical doctrines and not least those doctrines of which it is a part.

BEHAVIORISM AND PHYSICALISM

The behaviorist ideal was to describe and predict animal and human behavior without using so-called mentalist terms, and assuming in effect that only the animal's body and its movements were observable. The failure of this ideal and why it must fail is seen most easily in the case of verbal behavior, but the reasons why it fails in that case are the reasons why it must fail in the case of nonverbal behavior as well. If a so-called human being is a human body, his so-called actions are macro-movements of that body. But by the same token, his so-called utterances, assertions, questions and so on, will be vocalizations or sounds emitted orally from that body.

To call this *verbal* behavior would already imply that it was not just that. Though we certainly make sounds when we speak, making assertions, asking questions, or urging or commanding people to do things are not identical with vocalizing or making the sounds, nor is what we assert, ask, or command identical with the sounds we make. It is not even identical with the sentences we utter. One may utter an interrogative sentence without asking a question. But to identify a sentence as declarative, interrogative, or imperative is to identify it as a type of sentence commonly uttered in asserting, asking, urging, or commanding, and since these are intentional acts no less than any others, obviously there are no such sentences unless there are people, for only people ask questions, make assertions, or give orders. That they mean to do so goes without saying—these are not the kinds of things that people are apt to do accidentally or inadvertently or automatically (like breathing). And what people say (as distinct from their saying it) is generally what they mean to say, though they may very well not say all that they think and quite commonly mean more than they say. What they otherwise do is also generally what they mean to do, though it often does not have the intended result. What people mean or intend to do is manifest in what they do, just as what they mean to say is manifest in what they say. Intentions do not lurk secretly behind utterances and actions; they are normally manifest in them. What is often not clear is a person's motives and reasons—why he says what he says or does what he does. If what someone says is obscure, we want to know what he means (to say) and why, but what we demand is not insight or entry into his supposed mind, but elaboration and elucidation—we want him to say more. Similarly, if we do not understand what he is doing, short of asking him, we watch to see what else he does or we try to find out what he did or said earlier. To understand fragments of a text what we want is the rest of it, not something that lies or lay behind it.

A person may be said to intend to do something before he does it, and in such a case when it comes to the point he may not do what he intended. It may be this which has led some people to imagine that intentions are distinct and separate things from actions, just as it was formerly imagined that there were acts of will or volitions which were quite distinct from physical actions. Hence the claim that intentions, like acts of will, are unobservable. If what a person means to do were excluded from the domain of observation—and likewise therefore what he does unintentionally, accidentally, or inadvertently —intentions, if any, would then be hypothetical, unobservable mental events or states. But to stick to what was observable, one would then have not to listen to what a speaker says, but only to the sounds which are produced by his breath and vocal organs. A corresponding procedure in the case of what someone had written would be not to read it but just to look at the marks and groups of marks on the page. If intentions were posited as distinctive mental events *behind* behavior, as Quine and others have held, the sentences people uttered, the assertions they made, and the questions they asked would likewise have to be posited as distinctive things behind the sounds in the air or the marks on the page. Physicalists and behaviorists, however, do not generally think out what their doctrines would commit them to if they took them seriously, and of course none of them has attempted to act accordingly. It is not that it would be foolish to try, but that one cannot imagine what trying to act accordingly would consist of. What would a Berkeleyan do to demonstrate that he really did believe there was no matter? He has done all he can do in that line by professing the doctrine in his performances. So it is with physicalism. That is the way with metaphysical doctrines. The performances themselves could not be given if what is professed in them were true. Berkeley was of course a person, a man of flesh and blood, and could not have written a word had he not been. It follows that his professed immaterialism is false. But likewise any physicalist is of course a person and it is as such that he addresses us. It follows that physicalism is false. Consider this passage in which a physicalist addresses us:

> Mental entities are unobjectionable if conceived as hypothetical physical mechanisms and posited with a view strictly to the systematizing of physical phenomena. They should be posited in the hope of their submitting some day to full physical explanation in turn. One must not mistake the familiarity of mentalistic talk for clarity, and thus be tempted into a dream world of introspection.[14]

Is this itself a specimen of mentalistic talk? Are hopes and temptations mental entities? Are they conceived as hypothetical physical mechanisms? This is like the question whether Berkeley, when he denounces the notion or pseudo-notion of material substance, is merely denouncing Locke's something-we-know-not-what that stands under and supports the qualities, or whether he is denouncing the ordinary notion of stuff (gold or coal being kinds of stuff). Berkeley's own doctrine concerning coal and gold is that they are congeries of ideas without the Lockean idea of something-we-know-not-what. The ordinary notion of a stuff or substance is never denounced, though it is at odds equally with Locke's something and with Berkeley's nothing-we-know-not-what. As the context and "a dream world of introspection" make clear, Quine is rejecting any doctrine of ideas conceived as mental events or entities, just as Berkeley rejects Locke's something-we-know-not-what. But just as there is no Lockean substance talk outside the exposition of metaphysical doctrines, so there is no mentalistic talk of the kind Quine denounces outside of metaphysical performances. But what about the terms we actually use, terms such as Quine uses in this passage—"hoping," "mistaking," or "being tempted?" What kind of terms are they in Quine's doctrine? They have no status and belong to no doctrine, just like the ordinary notion of kinds of stuff. It is in these terms that Quine urges us to engage in his kind of performance and not that other kind. They are as irrelevant to what is professed in the performance as an actor's opinion of a play is to the character he is playing in the play. What Quine opposes to the dream world of introspection is not the real world in which *in propria persona* he urges us to renounce it but another dream world which, still *in propria persona*, he bids us enter or assures us we may enter in time.

> When we quote a man's utterance directly we report it almost as we might a bird call. However significant the utterance, direct quotation merely reports the physical incident and leaves any implication to us. On the other hand in indirect quotation we project ourselves into what, from his remarks and other indications, we imagine the speaker's state of mind to have been, and then we say what, in our language, is natural and relevant for us in the state thus feigned. An indirect quotation we can usually expect to rate only as better or worse, more or less faithful, and we cannot even hope for a strict standard of more or less; what is involved is evaluation, relative to special pur-

poses, of an essentially dramatic act. Correspondingly for the other propositional attitudes, for all of them can be thought of as involving something like quotation of one's own imagined verbal response to an imagined situation.[15]

This account of what we do when we use indirect quotation is a version of a traditional story about how we come to ascribe thoughts, beliefs, feelings, attitudes, intentions, and so on, to others, when we have only the movements of bodies and sounds emitted from mouths to go on. The assumption is that these are secret mental things that can only be ascribed to others by analogy with one's own case—the traditional and notoriously unsuccessful answer to the problem of solipsism. Again in the traditional way, Quine backs up his story by reference to our descriptions of what dumb animals are up to:

Casting ourselves thus into unreal roles, we do not generally know how much reality to hold constant. Quandaries arise. But despite them we find ourselves attributing beliefs, wishes, and strivings even to creatures lacking the power of speech, such is our dramatic virtuosity. We project ourselves even into what from his behavior we imagine a mouse's state of mind to have been, and dramatize it as a belief, wish, or striving, verbalized as seems relevant and natural to us in the state thus feigned.[16]

If we could not ascribe beliefs, wishes, and strivings to other people without putting ourselves in their shoes, we could not do so to other animals without putting ourselves in their shoes. But since to project oneself is to verbalize as seems relevant and natural in the state thus feigned, and other creatures cannot verbalize—nor therefore *know* that they are in any state—to predicate with Burns a panic in the breastie of the beastie is mere dramatic virtuosity or fiction, and just a short step from the adventures of Mickey Mouse. To be in a state or to try to do anything is to be able to verbalize accordingly. A mouse therefore cannot be in a panic or try to reach the cheese unless it knows the words "panic" and "cheese" and perhaps "Cheddar" and "Camembert." Since we freely apply A-predicates* to other animals as well as to human beings, we must be imagining what it would be like to be a mouse, a dog, or an elephant, as the

*See p. 58.

case may be. But a dog plainly loves eating stuff that to us would be disgusting—imagine eating it and the gorge rises.

It is not clear how Quine thinks direct quotation is like reporting a bird call. But this remark does invite consideration of how reports and descriptions of human behavior differ from reports and descriptions of the behavior of other animals. One obvious difference is speech behavior. To report it at all, we cannot report it as we would a bird call or any other type of behavior in other animals. The difference is this. We can report a crow's call or cry in various ways—"The crow uttered a cry," "The crow cawed in alarm," or " 'Caw-aw! Caw-aw!' cried the crow," and in this last form we attempt to imitate the cry or use a conventional imitation. Compare this with " 'The man is an idiot!' cried Harry." Here we are not imitating Harry's cry but saying what he cried, and what he cried is simply what he said in a vehement manner. In the sense in which we report what Harry cried, we do not report what the crow cried, for there is no such thing to report. The crow uttered a cry, but Harry did not utter a cry. Harry uttered words, and indeed a sentence. Harry's vocalizations and the crow's cries are of course equally physical incidents—both of them made or emitted sounds. But what Harry said is not a mere physical incident. We cannot hear what Harry is saying unless we know the language he is speaking. Also we must be near enough to make out what he is saying, and various other conditions must be fulfilled. We may hear Harry speaking, the sounds of Harry's voice, in the next room or through a hubbub of other sounds, but not hear what he is saying. Only if we do hear what he says can we report it. Otherwise we can only report that he spoke. But even this reports more than a mere physical incident. Now unless his words are ambiguous, as countless sentences are when we do not know the context and situation of the speaker, we know what he said, and this in the normal case is what he meant to say. If the projection story were true, we should have to project ourselves into his imagined state of mind even to understand what he meant to say. But of course we do not—other people say quite surprising things and sometimes things that leave us aghast, but we understand perfectly what they mean. In reporting without verbatim notes what someone said, there are two reasons why direct quotation is unusual except in short snatches. The first is that it is hard to recall a person's words but easy to recall what he said. That is one of the reasons

Quine gives why indirect quotation is here to stay—it is "humanly indispensable." The other is that common speech is truncated and can hardly be understood without knowledge of the context and practical situation of the speakers. People do not say all that they mean the listener to understand, especially among familiars. Direct quotation might well come out as gibberish.

Quine's doctrine would forbid the distinction between the sounds a person makes, the words he utters, and what he says—what assertions he makes, what instructions he gives, what questions he asks, and so on. If anything is merely physical, it is the sounds or sound waves. Since Quine's interest is in language, not sounds, he cannot go the whole hog, and he therefore settles for the words uttered and calls that the physical incident. His objection to indirect quotation arises from his objection to mentalism and to the projection story which he believes to be essential to mentalism—rightly so, for in mentalist doctrine there is a problem of solipsism and something like the projection story is required. Quine's doubts concerning paraphrase, his objection to the notion of saying the same thing or expressing the same idea in different words, and of course to the notion of a proposition, all have the same source. He just fails to observe that ordinary discourse about people and other animals is not mentalist.

But to use direct quotation *is* to report what a person said and not just to report the words he uttered. The idea of direct quotation is to quote a speaker's very words, but we can do this only if he is saying something—making an assertion, asking a question, giving instructions, telling a story, and so on. If a person recites a poem, he of course utters the words of the poem, but he is not himself saying anything. There is no such thing here as quoting *his* very words, for the very words he utters in that order are not *his* words. Similarly, an actor playing Hamlet speaks the words or the lines of the part he has learned, but what Hamlet says in the play is not what the actor says. The actor does not say he is a rogue and peasant slave—even if he thinks he is. It is Hamlet in the play who says that. The actor speaks Hamlet's words but himself says nothing.

There is nothing analogous to direct quotation in reporting nonverbal behavior. But nonverbal behavior and the nonverbal context and situation are usually essential to understanding, if not what a person says, at least why he says it. In Quine's account, only reports of the words a person uttered are immune to the ills of projection and dramatic virtuosity, for if these ills arise in indirect reporting of people's utterances, they must arise *a fortiori* in reporting their non-verbal behavior. Behavior, verbal and nonverbal, can be described or reported—and truly—in many different ways. But not every true description is the right kind of description, and not every description of the right kind is true. There is a fundamental reason why descriptions that come naturally are the right kind even when they are false. They are the ones which are informed by our unarticulated knowledge of practices, institutions, roles, trades, techniques, customs, manners, milieux, morals, types of social relations, and much else. It is in the light of this enormous body of knowledge that we understand the diverse and sometimes highly original ploys of individuals. Sympathy or empathy doubtless counts in our evaluation or judgment of these ploys, but we can perfectly well know what a person is up to and understand his motives without it.

"If we are limning the true and ultimate structure of reality, the canonical scheme for us is the austere scheme that knows no quotation but direct quotation and no propositional attitudes but only the physical constitution and behavior of organisms."[17] The canonical scheme is one that eliminates failure of substitutivity *salva veritate*,* which arises with so-called verbs of propositional attitude like "believe." Thus in Quine's example, "Philip believes that Tegucigalpa is the capital of Nicaragua" may be true and "Philip believes that the capital of Honduras is the capital of Nicaragua," may be false, though Tegucigalpa and the capital of Honduras are the same city. The same goes for "Philip knows . . ." and "Philip says . . ." Thus "Philip knows that the capital of Honduras is not the capital of Nicaragua" may be true but "Philip knows that Tegucigalpa is not the capital of Nicaragua" may be false.[18] Though failure of substitutivity occurs in other contexts, this is the type of context in which reference to people is essential. Eliminate such contexts and reference to intentional agents is eliminated.

Quine agrees that the "the intentional does not reduce and that it is at least in a practical way indispensable."[19] His use of "intentional" is not the ordinary one, though it is related. A verb like "believe"

---

*If two expressions designate the same thing, to substitute the one for the other in a sentence should make no difference to the truth, but in contexts such as the one cited, one sentence may be true and the other false. This is called failure of substitutivity *salva veritate* (with truth preserved).

is in his sense an intentional verb and objects of so-called propositional attitudes like believing are intentional objects. "To intend" and "to mean" are themselves intentional verbs in this sense, and the intended result of an action is an intentional object in the same sense, though it is not a proposition. There are countless other intentional verbs like "trying to," "proposing to," and so on. Thus one may in golf intend to drive or try to drive from the eighteenth tee to the green, but not intend to drive or try to drive 350 yards in a south-southwesterly direction, though driving to the green and driving that distance in that direction from the tee are the same thing. Similarly with verbs of perception: I may see a man at the end of the street but not my old friend Harry, though the man I see is my old friend Harry. This illustrates a point often made about stimulus objects in stimulus-response theory: it is not the mere object to which the animal responds but the object as it is perceived. Some people say "the object under a certain description," though other animals cannot describe anything and cannot identify anything by a term or description. But of course they can and must recognize kinds of things. Obviously monkeys recognize bananas and know what bananas are like, though they do not know what bananas are, that is, what "bananas" or some corresponding expression means. If we may speak of intentional objects at all, we may do so in the case of other animals as well as ourselves.

In the ordinary sense only actions are intentional or unintentional. What one does intentionally is what one does on purpose or what one means to do, by contrast with what one does without meaning to, accidentally or inadvertently, or by contrast with what one does automatically or mechanically (as one moves one's tongue in speaking) or by reflex (as one blinks or jumps when startled). No doubt many other animals also act intentionally, but people surely do.

NOTES

1. P. F. Strawson, *Individuals* (London: Methuen, 1959), p. 104.
2. Ibid., p. 89.
3. Ibid., p. 103.
4. Ibid., p. 115.
5. Locke, *Essay*, Book II, Ch. XXVII, p. 281.
6. Strawson, *Individuals*, p. 115.
7. Ibid., p. 90.

8. Ibid., p. 83.

9. Ibid., p. 115.

10. Ibid.

11. Ibid., p. 116.

12. *Enquiry*, pp. 64-65.

13. Ibid., p. 66.

14. W. V. Quine, *The Roots of Reference* (LaSalle, Ill.: Open Court, 1973), pp. 33-34.

15. W. V. Quine, *Word and Object* (Cambridge, Mass.: MIT Press, 1960), p. 219.

16. Ibid.

17. Ibid., p. 121.

18. W. V. Quine, "Reference and Modality," in *From a Logical Point of View* (Cambridge, Mass.: Harvard University Press, 1953) p. 141.

19. Quine, *Word and Object*, pp. 221-22.

Part Two

Linguistic Transcendentalism

4

Universals and Abstract Objects

The notion of a universal and with it the celebrated problem of universals was invented by Plato. Nominalism in its various forms is no less a doctrine of universals than realism, and a good example of the fact that metaphysical doctrines feed from the hands they bite. The distinction of particulars and universals is complemented in many doctrines since Plato with the distinction and division of labor between the senses and the reason or intellect, or understanding. According to these doctrines, what is given to the bodily senses is merely particular, and the understanding or reason alone apprehends, or constructs or derives, the universal. Many philosophers take the problem of universals to be that of the meaning of general terms without realizing that what makes the meaning of general terms a problem is the very concept of a universal.

In countless doctrines, the ordinary concept of a sort, type, or kind of thing in any category is simply ignored. If this seems astonishing, it is no more so than the neglect of the everyday concept of a human being or animal—a visible, tangible, ponderable entity that feels, thinks, and perceives—in discussions of the so-called mind-body problem by dualists and materialists alike. Since it is not possible to think at all without the concept of a sort, kind, or type of thing, the authors of doctrines with which this concept is incompatible have employed it even as they advanced these doctrines. The concepts of a property and of a concept itself are not quite in the same boat—they have not been so much ignored. But doctrinal accounts of them are also commonly incompatible with the ways in which they are used in these very accounts. But again this should not surprise anyone who has considered Berkeley's use of stuff terms in the course of expounding a doctrine that denies stuff. There are many other examples of the same thing.

For the present I am not concerned with the distinction of species, breeds, and varieties of animals or plants, nor of natural kinds and social, conventional, or artificial kinds, but just with the distinction between a kind, or sort, or type and a particular or token. (It is obvious that stallions, mares, foals, fillies, geldings, yearlings, and the like are types of horse, but not species or breeds of horse.)

If one points to some visible object and asks "What is that?" the question can have either of two senses. If one is pointing to a building in plain view, the question will be what particular building it is, and an appropriate answer will be something like "The Bank of Scotland" or "Younger's Brewery." But if one is pointing to something in the distance or to some unfamiliar object nearby, the sense of the question will be "What kind of thing is that?" and an appropriate answer will be something like "It's a tree," "It's a sculpture," or "It's a generator." Similarly, if one points to a building and says "That is one of my favorite buildings," the demonstrative "that" will refer to one particular building. But if one points to a flower and says "That is one of my favorite flowers," the word "that" will normally refer to the species or variety of flower, of which the present one is a specimen. One may also point to a particular rose and say "That kind is my favorite" or "I love that kind of rose." These examples are enough to show that the referent of a direct demonstrative is often a type, sort, or kind of thing.

But it is often asserted or supposed that in demonstrative reference to something in view or in earshot what is referred to must be a particular and only a particular thing. This view is cognate with the classic dogma of empiricists and rationalists alike that what is given to the senses is merely particular, on which the Cartesian doctrine of innate ideas is partly founded, and with the empiricist and nominalist doctrine that whatever exists is particular. This latter doctrine, if it means anything, entails that there are no kinds of things. But in fact one could not see a particular rose if one could not see the kind of thing it was. It is indeed inconceivable that one should see or spot one of a kind but not the kind of one. Of course one does not see two things, the particular and the kind. In the sense in which a particular rose is a thing, the kind of thing it is, is not a thing: all things in that sense are particular things, not kinds. But *what* a particular is, is the kind of thing it is. *Which* one it is, is the very particular one—the pen in my hand, the rose in my button-hole, or whatever. In many cases, it is a matter of indifference whether one refers to a particular or to the kind: "This creature is a spider," "This kind of creature is a spider." "Spider" in any case signifies the kind it is, a visible, recognizable kind. A spider is one of that kind or that kind of one.

The open sentence "*x* is a spider" determines a class only because "spider" signifies a kind of thing. It is by being one of that kind or that kind of one that a value of *x* is a member of the class. To identify something as a spider, one must know what a spider is, that is, what kind of thing "spider" signifies. Kinds of things can come to be or cease to be. The chemical elements, kinds of substances, are believed to have evolved. The motorbike—the kind of vehicle known as a motorbike—was invented about 1880. The dodo is extinct. There is no obvious way of producing statements equivalent to these in terms of classes. The class of dodos and the class of dead dodos are not identical: though all dodos are dead, a dead dodo is not a dodo, but, if anything remains, the mortal remains of one.

Since a kind is to be found wherever there are particular things of the kind, it can have various geographical locations. The lion is found in East Africa. Lions are found in East Africa. It makes no difference whether we say "the lion" or whether we say "lions": what is meant is the kind of animal. To say that it can be seen in captivity far from its remaining natural habitats does not contradict the statement that it is found in East Africa. A kind is not a class: the class of lions is nowhere to be found. Similarly, the horse is an animal used for riding or draught, which was first domesticated in Central Asia. These statements do not entail that no horses are wild. We need never speak of the horse, but only of horses; but we are still speaking of the kind, not the class. If the claim that everything that exists is particular means anything at all, it entails that there are no horses, no lions, and no people, for these are all kinds of thing or being, and a kind is not a particular. Those who advanced that celebrated doctrine simply deceived themselves. Unless there are kinds of things, one could not ask "What's that over there?" for this usually means "What kind of thing is that over there?"

In Quine's *Word and Object* and earlier works, no acknowledgment is to be found of the notion of kinds or sorts, though he often uses the words, and his essay on natural kinds in *Ontological Relativity* is not about kinds but about similarity, which he takes to be the same thing. According to his doctrine in *Word and Object,* however, to be is to be an entity or object, and objects are of two broad *kinds,* concrete and abstract. Of abstract objects, Quine would like to make do with one kind, classes. Of concrete objects, there are at least two kinds, scattered ones like red, blue, soap, and toffee, and compact ones like lumps of coal and us. Since all objects of whatever kind are particular objects, and to be is to be an object, the answer to the question what general terms mean ought to be either that there is nothing for them to mean or that the question is a pseudo-question. According to Quine, general terms are true or false of objects, but why they are true or false, what makes them true or false, is left in obscurity. In "Two Dogmas" and in *Word and Object* they are said to be meaningful or significant. But so is any word that makes any difference to the sense of a sentence, and that includes, besides general terms, "if," "and," "some," and all other syncategorematic terms, i.e., terms that do not mean some kind of thing.

Quine considered the idea that a general term meant *something* to be based on a confusion of sense and reference. "What sort of things are meanings?" he asked in *Two Dogmas* (note the use of "sort"). "A felt need for meant entities may derive from an earlier failure to appreciate that meaning and reference are distinct. Once the theory of meaning is sharply separated from the theory of reference, it is a short step to recognizing as the primary business of the theory of meaning simply the synonymy of linguistic forms and the analyticity of statements; meanings themselves as obscure intermediary entities may well be abandoned."[1] A general term on this view can be meaningful, but there is nothing that it means nor something—viz., a meaning—that it has. There are no "supposititious entities called meanings."[2] Meaningfulness thus appears to be internal to a word or expression and has no connection with anything extralinguistic that we come across.

A simple example will show the contrary. The senses of the two sentences "Tom went to the meeting on a motorbike" and "Tom went to the meeting on a horse" are different, and what makes the difference is obviously the final word in each sentence. How do they differ, besides by being different words? They mean or signify two different kinds of thing, and it is only because they do that the senses of the two sentences are different. Their semantic role or, in other words, the contribution each makes to the sense of the sentence in which it occurs, is just to signify a kind of thing. There is no confusion here of sense and reference. "Tom" refers to a person. It is of Tom that something is predicated. It is senseless to ask what "Tom" means; all one can ask is who Tom is, whom "Tom" names, or what the referent of "Tom" is. But it is not senseless to ask what "motorbike" means. An answer consists of some more or less useful description of a motorbike, the sort of thing it means, the sort of thing that any motorbike is. This is what one finds in all practical dictionaries—not synonyms. For obvious reasons only a dud dictionary would give "motorcycle" as the definition of "motorbike." A similar account can be given of the difference in sense of the two sentences "Tom walked to the meeting" and "Tom ran to the meeting": the two verbs mean or signify two different types of natural human locomotion. So there is something that general terms mean whether they be nouns, adjectives, verbs, or adverbs: kinds of thing, kinds of action, types of quality, property, and so on.

Consider this passage from Michael Dummett's book on Gottlob Frege:

> The fundamental question of ontology is "What is there?" where, of course, since an actual inventory is not required, the intention of the question is "What kinds of things are there?" How the question is broken down then depends upon the basic principles of categorization. On the traditional conception, the first step towards breaking it down consists of specializing to the two questions, "What particulars are there?" and "Are there universals, and, if so, what universals are there?" where of course the second question raises the problem of nominalism as traditionally conceived. The question, "What objects are there?" on the other hand, arises only against the background of a Fregean ontological perspective, and its companions are, "Are there concepts?" "Are there relations?" "Are there functions?" and "Are there truth values?" The question about objects may be broken down further into ones concerning concrete objects and abstract objects.[3]

If the ontological question is "What kinds of things are there?" then if there is anything at all there must be kinds of things in the loose noncategorial sense of "thing." The concept of a kind and the concept of a particular must be fundamental in any account of what there is and in any account of the semantics of any language in which people speak about what there is. The ontological question assumes the existence of kinds and particular things. But one cannot both make or assume that distinction and regard particulars as one kind of thing and kinds of thing as another kind of thing. Neither "particular" nor "kind" are themselves generic or sortal terms: they do not themselves signify any kind of thing. Take a horse, Dobbin: Dobbin is certainly a particular and certainly a kind of particular. But to say he is a particular is not to say what kind of thing he is, and to say he is a kind of particular is still not to say what kind of thing he is. To say he is a horse is certainly to do just that, likewise a mammal, an animal, and a material being, in the first category distinguished by Aristotle, and therefore not a property, relation, action, etc. The ordinary kind of category mistake consists of assigning things in crude or subtle ways to the wrong category or taking what a term signifies to be in one category when it is in another. But it is a fundamental and deep category mistake to regard particulars as one kind of thing and kinds of thing as another kind of thing. But this is what countless philosophers have done and still do. Nominalists essentially deny the existence of the second of these two supposed kinds of things. If particulars and kinds were two different kinds of things, then man (a kind of animal), blue (a type of color), brotherhood (a type of relation), and granite (a kind of rock) would all be one kind of thing, and Socrates, blue spots, the brotherhood of Henry and William James, and granite rocks would all be another kind of thing. But they are not. Neither "kind" nor "particular" signifies any kind of thing. The fundamental, indispensable distinction of kind and particular is not a distinction of kinds.

If kinds and particulars were two kinds of entity, since it is kinds that can be predicated, particulars could be predicated as well as kinds. Since they cannot, it follows that these are not two kinds of entity. If kinds were things or entities and particulars a different kind of thing or entity, neither one a species of the other, whenever one spotted a beetle one would spot not only two different entities but two different kinds of entity, the particular and the kind, and it would be natural to ask how they were related. But of course one does not. One spots one thing, a beetle, a thing of a certain kind. Aristotle got this right.

At the beginning of his chapter on abstract objects, Dummett asserts that the notion of an object introduced by Frege makes a clean break with the tradition still represented by Strawson, according to which, in Dummett's words, "entities are to be categorized as particulars and universals."[4] Certainly this is an ancient tradition descending from Plato. According to it, there are two categories or kinds of entity, particulars and universals. Hence we have the explicit distinction between a particular and a universal, and the one that is casually taken for granted in stating this distinction, the one between an entity and a kind or category. Are these one and the same distinction or are they different? It is hard to see what the distinction between a kind and an entity could be but the familiar one between a kind and a particular. Either the distinction between a universal and a particular must also be the same one, or else it must be a distinction between two kinds of particular. If universals are the same as kinds, since the distinction of kind and particular is not a distinction of kinds, the distinction of universal and particular is not a distinction of kinds either. If it is a distinction of kinds, it must be a distinction of kinds of particular.

In the traditional doctrine, says Dummett, universals can be referred to or they can be predicated of particulars or of other universals, whereas particulars can be referred to but not predicated of anything. Since it is kinds or types of entity, property, relation, activity, and the like which are predicated of particulars and of other kinds, this version clearly identifies universals with kinds.

Though the term "universal" comes from Latin and was meant to translate Aristotle's nominalization of an adjectival or adverbial expression *katholou,* the concept was invented by Plato. Ideas or Forms in Plato's philosophy are clearly conceived as supratemporal or eternal particulars, and it is from this that the problem of their relation to ordinary temporal particulars, as well as to each other, arises. If they were kinds, there would be no such problem. There is no problem with the adjective "universal." Nominalists were certainly right to deny the existence of Platonic universals, but the nominalist claim that only particulars exist is itself compatible with the claim that universals exist, for they are conceived as atemporal, suprasensible particulars. But philosophers who speak about universals continually lapse into thinking of them as kinds.

In the traditional doctrine, according to which one can both refer to universals and predicate them of particulars and of other universals, a general term like "lion" would signify or designate a universal. This universal would be predicated of a particular in such a sentence as "This is a lion" and referred to in such a sentence as "The lion is a creature of the cat family." The lion being carnivorous and subject, I believe, to melancholy in captivity, that universal would be carnivorous and subject to melancholy. And just as one can point to an animal and say "this kind" or "this species," so one should be able to point to one and say "This universal comes from East Africa." Only if "universal" were a synonym of "type or "sort" or "species" would this make sense, but even then one would have to admit expressions like "This universal of animal," "This universal of rose is my favorite." But clearly "universal" is not admissible in such contexts, and this shows that the logical syntax is quite different from that of "kind," "sort," type," "species," and so on. No such problem arises from the philosophical use of "particular" as a noun. There is no logical difficulty in referring to a particular animal as "this particular." But the notion of a universal is that of a peculiar kind of particular and that is why it makes no sense in any of these contexts.

Many people have tried in their metaphysical performances, consciously or half consciously to avoid such nonsense by referring, for example, to the universal which is allegedly predicated in "This beast is a lion," by the expression "lionhood." Many similar malformations occur in philosophical writings—*doghood, thinghood, eventhood,* and so on. They are formed by mistaken analogy with *manhood, womanhood, girlhood, widowhood, bachelorhood,* and of course not with *neighborhood, hardihood, falsehood, likelihood,* or *Little Red Riding Hood.* The story is that in such a sentence as "Tom is a man" manhood is ascribed to or predicated of Tom. But manhood is the mature or adult state of a male human being. The kind of thing signified by "man" is not a type of state but a kind of being—an adult being certainly but a being, not a state. The prime candidates for the status of universals have indeed been types of state, condition, disposition, and quality, and not types of beings or material things. They have been things like courage, justice, wisdom, red, and so on. These are clearly not particulars but types of virtue, disposition, quality, and so on. The noun "universal" is at best useless.

Now Dummett claims that Frege's notion of an object makes

a clean break with the tradition according to which there are two basic kinds of things, particulars and universals. I think Aristotle made such a break with Plato, but not Frege. "Questions such as whether or not there are any abstract objects," says Dummett, "what abstract objects there are and how we know they exist, what is the criterion for their existence, where the dividing line comes between concrete and abstract objects—all these are modern questions."[5] Though the expression "abstract object" is a modern expression, this claim is surely mistaken. Most of the problems are the old familiar problems of universals with some new, equally insoluble problems added.

An object in the Fregean doctrine is the referent of a proper name, of a demonstrative expression like "that man over there" or of some other expression that is not a predicate. This is Dummett's own view and also Quine's. On this view, according to Dummett, "terms (proper names) and predicates are expressions of such radically different kinds, that is, play such radically different roles in the language, that it is senseless to suppose that the same thing could be alluded to both by some predicate and by some term."[6] The reason for using the verb "to allude" here is, I suppose, to avoid using "to refer," "to mention," or "to mean." On the Fregean view, according to Dummett, "we can do nothing with the suggestion that a certain term—say, 'wisdom'—should be regarded as standing for the very same thing as that which a certain predicate—in this case 'x is wise'—stands for."[7] We can indeed do nothing with that suggestion; whatever the sense of "stands for," one cannot think what "x is wise" could be said to stand for. But the obvious and correct suggestion is that the noun "wisdom" and the adjective "wise" signify the same virtue and that the difference in their use is not semantic but syntactic. According to Dummett, if we reconstrue "Wisdom is not confined to the old" as "Not only the old are wise," we deny the status of a genuine term or proper name to "wisdom." If wisdom were a universal or Idea—a suprasensible, atemporal particular—then "wisdom" would be its proper name in English. Similarly, if it were a so-called abstract object. Only if one supposes that it could be this will one speak of reconstruing. But "Not only the old are wise" is obviously a close, exact paraphrase of "Wisdom is not confined to the old." The only way to determine if there is any difference of sense is to see if you can detect any. If there were any, there would also be a difference between "The old are wise" and "The old have wisdom," and between the "The old are very wise" and "The old have great wisdom," and likewise between "Mary is very beautiful" and "Mary has great beauty." But being wise is identical with having wisdom, and being beautiful with having beauty. The adjective and the noun in each case signify the same attribute. In these and in many other (but not all) cases, "has" followed by the noun gives the same sense as "is" followed by the adjective. "To have" in such contexts has no passive voice. It is not a relational, transitive verb. There are of course other contexts in which it is, notably when it has the sense of "to own." But "to possess" can also be nonrelational: "Mary possesses great beauty" is just a fancy way of saying she has great beauty or is very beautiful.

In Quine's doctrine, attributes, if there are any, are abstract objects, values of individual variables no less than cows. They are referents of what he calls abstract singular terms, whereas cows are referents of concrete ones. Such abstract objects are not of course posited *ad lib.,* in his doctrine, but, according to Quine's own view, they *are* posited *ad lib.,* in other doctrines and in the language of everyday discourse in English. But in plain English, attributes are characteristics, properties, or qualities that things have. Thus if a thing is flexible, it has flexibility, or, in other words, one of its attributes or properties is flexibility. If "flexibility" were an abstract singular term, however, and flexibility an abstract object, anything that had flexibility would have an abstract object, and to ask what properties a thing had would be to ask what its abstract objects were.

Whereas "round" and the like play the role of "F" in "Fa," "roundness" and the like are suited rather to the role of "a" or "b" in "Fa," "Fab," etc. Now in order for this latter role to exist for abstract singular terms, there have to be some abstract general terms for the supporting role of "F": some general terms predicable of abstract objects. Two such abstract general terms are "virtue" and "rare": thus "Fa" can be "Humility is a virtue" or "Humility is rare." Again a relative term that is abstract at one end is "has," as in "a has humility" or "a has roundness," which have the form "Fab." The move that ushers in abstract singular terms has to be one that simultaneously ushers in abstract general ones.[8]

Since there is at most a rhetorical nuance of difference between "Tom is humble" and "Tom has humility" or between "Tom is very humble" and "Tom has great humility," the form for both is obviously "Fa." "Has" is no more a relative term in the one case than "is" in the other. But this plain, natural, and obviously correct view of the matter is an example of what Quine calls "that facile line of thought."

> For I deplore that facile line of thought according to which we may freely use abstract terms, in all the ways in which terms are used without thereby acknowledging the existence of any abstract objects. According to this counsel, abstract turns of phrase are mere linguistic usage innocent of metaphysical commitment to a peculiar realm of entities . . . . If idioms ostensibly about abstract objects are to be defended as linguistic conveniences, why not see this defense as a defense of the reifications in the only possible sense?[9]

Since some essential dogmas of his doctrine are embodied in the key terms, "abstract object," "abstract singular term," and "reification," he begs the question and appears not to understand the facile line of thought. The facile line is not that "abstract turns of phrase are mere linguistic usage." The facile line is just that the noun "humility" is not an abstract singular term or proper name of an abstract object, but just a general term like "humble" signifying the same state or disposition, and that this is why "has" with the noun and "is" with the adjective are synonymous in this and many similar cases. Similarly, "Humility is rare" means no more and no less than "Few people are humble" or "Few have humility." There is no reification of anything that is not in fact a *res* or *thing* and none therefore to be defended. If humility were an abstract object, it is not clear how one abstract object could be rare or common any more than one concrete object—one man or one horse—or what the sense of injunctions like "Have some humility" would be. The facile line of thought being rejected, why not treat humility as a scattered concrete object like water and red, and interpret "Have some humility" on the same lines as "Have some tea"?

Consider the question "What color is the book?" You may prefer "What is the color of the book?" But the sense is exactly the same. To reply to the question in the first form with "The book is not a color. No book is a color" is a poor joke. We find the same idiom in "The book is not red but some other color"; "What other color could it be?"; "James was the color of a beetroot"; "The garden is the length of a football field"; "The garden and the football field are the same length"; "James's friend is the size of an ox"; "His aunt is the shape of a pumpkin." These are all grammatically normal sentences. In each of them a noun phrase is used adjectivally and can be paraphrased out, without loss or gain of sense. What this shows is that a noun phrase like "the color of a beetroot" and an adjective like "beetroot" meaning "beetroot-colored" signify the same color, and since they do, "is" readily replaces the more formal "has."

The way we trace the line of demarcation between abstract and concrete objects, says Dummett, depends in part on the "fine structure" of our language.[10] If the senses of "having" belong to the fine structure, however, this fine structure forbids our regarding many alleged abstract objects as objects at all: such objects would have to be, like universals, a peculiar kind of particular. If virtues (like humility) or vices (like envy) were objects, people could have them only in the sense in which Mary had a little lamb or in some other relational sense. But that is not the sense and they are therefore not objects. The same goes for qualities like color. To have a certain color, such as red, is just to *be red.*

Also mistaken is the view that general terms for kinds of stuff are proper names when they occur in the subject position in a sentence, that they are what Quine calls abstract singular terms. Dummett, discussing Saul Kripke's account of naming, remarks that "water" in "Water is a compound" is used as a proper name but "is rather differently used in 'Give me a glass of water,' 'He fell into some water,' and the like."[11] But if water is the kind of stuff that "water" names, a glass of water is clearly a glass of the kind of stuff that "water" names. If "water" were a proper name in the first sentence, it would be a proper name in the second, too. And if someone fell into some water, he would fall into some of the kind of stuff that "water" names. It clearly makes no sense to speak of falling into some of an object or of having a glass of some object. The concept of an object will not fit water or any kind of stuff, nor any sort in *any* category. It will *only* fit particulars.

At one point, Dummett notices that a so-called abstract object is in fact a sort or type, but then it appears with some surprise. He first takes chess, chess openings, and chess moves to be abstract objects, unperturbed by the consequence that some objects can be played or made again and again. "When taken as a type, not a token, a move in chess, such as Castling King's side or 1. P—K4 . . ., is surely an abstract object: yet we should feel little oddity about the use of a demonstrative as in 'What is that move called?' or 'Is that move to be recommended?' even when it was quite clear that 'move' was being used in a type and not a token sense."[12] In point of fact there is no oddity at all. The oddity arises only if one wrongly regards a type or kind of anything whatever as an object. "Move" does not have two senses, type and token. It is a general term signifying the same thing, whether "that move" refers to a type or to a token of the type, just as "rose" does in "That rose is my favorite." When such an expression as "that rose" refers to a particular, the general term "rose" signifies the kind of thing the particular is, *what* it is as opposed to which one.

One always feels a little crass in pointing out what everyone knows. Dummett's consideration of a chess move is what I have called, borrowing from Jean-Paul Sartre, a wakening in his perform-ance, like Berkeley's noting how strange it is to say that we eat and drink ideas. Dummett—and Berkeley or Descartes for that matter —is at such moments, like a dreamer on the point of waking and realizing that it is a dream, but then relapsing into the dream.

Dummett discusses various possible criteria for distinguishing an object as abstract, and among the candidates for this status are col-ors and shapes. Abstract objects, like Platonic universals, are not the kinds of things we can come across, encounter, or be shown, and they are not supposed to interact causally with other objects or to play any role in causal interactions. This seems at once to rule out colors and shapes. But the shape of an elephant's trunk, for example, is plainly visible and is of vital importance in its interactions with air, food, and water: it is essential to its functions that it taper towards the opening and not widen like a blunderbuss. Dummett recognizes a similar point regarding color. But he does so only to wrap the matter in ever deeper, though more intriguing, obscurity. If we accept the popular belief that a red rag provokes a bull, he says, there is no reason why we should not say the color causes the bull to charge, "but this is because we are not regarding a color as an abstract object and therefore allowing it to have spatial position, contingently. We can explain the bull's charge by the fact that the color was there, where he could see it."[13] If color were just a matter of how we regard it, why should we ever regard it as an abstract object? Dummett continues:

> Contrast the theory that the taste of a substance is determined by the shape of the molecules. Could we say that a certain shape causes a bitter taste? In so far as we regard a shape as a *genuine* abstract object, and therefore as not having, in itself, a spatial position, but merely as enjoying the property of being the shape of this or that configuration, we are reluctant to say this: the taste resulted, not from the presence of the shape, but from the presence of a molecule of that shape. . . .[14]

A red placard might be expected to provoke a bull just as well as a red rag, if it were indeed the color that mattered, whereas nothing but the shape of certain *molecules* would cause the taste. But just as it is the color of the rag or the placard that matters, so, according to the theory, it is the shape of the molecules that matters. There is no contrast.

What Dummett calls a "genuine abstract object," such as a shape, is exactly like a Platonic Form—it has, *in itself,* no spatial or temporal location and cannot therefore delimit an area or volume of stuff. But whereas the problem of the Forms was their relation to or connection with the characteristics of spatiotemporal things, this problem is buried in a piece of pure verbalism by Dummett, but verbalism of a very common kind in metaphysical performances. We simply regard the abstract object as "enjoying the property of being the shape of this or that object."[15] If "enjoying the property of being the shape of this or that object" had a clear sense, it would be the same as "being the shape of this or that object." A shape is indeed the shape of every object that has it, but all this means is that every object that has it, has it, not that it has some property. There is no passive voice of "to have" such that one might say the shape was had by the things that had it. Things can be had only in one or other of the relational senses of "to have." That several things have a certain shape does not entail that the shape has some property but simply that these things are so-shaped.

The delusion arises from the one we noted before, which is common to many metaphysical doctrines: that there are two basic kinds of things or entities, abstract and concrete, or universals and particulars, wisdom and wise people, the shape of a cube (or the Cube) and cubical things, red and red things. If wise people have wisdom, "have" must on this view be a relational term signifying their relation to this abstract object or universal, but if there is no distinction of sense between "Tom has wisdom" and "Tom is wise"—and there clearly is not—"is" must also be a relational term. Whatever the relation may be, it is impossible for wisdom to have no relation to the beings that are so related to it. So the relation it has to this or that wise person is a contingent characteristic of it, or as Dummett puts it, a property of it.

The concept of a property is regularly and grossly abused as a matter of course in countless philosophical arguments, many of which would just disintegrate and vanish without this abuse. In the wider sense, a property is any attribute or characteristic, but in the narrower and more usual sense the properties of a thing or substance are the ways in which it acts or reacts under various conditions. But both "attribute" and "property" are often used to mean whatever is predicated of, or ascribed to, a subject in the predicate of a sentence. So is "predicate." Hence it is that many philosophers assume that, for example, a man has the property of being a man, a cow of being a cow, and any particular of being a particular, and so on. But to be a man is to be a certain kind of being, not to have a certain property. The kind of being one is, is not a property one has. Nor is self-identity a property: nothing has itself as one of its properties. As "impredicable" is defined in the well-known paradox, a property is impredicable when it does not belong to itself, that is, when it does not have itself as a property or have the property that it is. It is assumed that some properties can and do have themselves, and also that predicability and impredicability are properties. Hence if impredicability belongs to itself it does not, and if it does not, it does. But all properties are impredicable, and impredicability is not a property. Belonging to something—being *had* by something—is *not* a property of any property, nor is not belonging to something.

NOTES

1. W. V. Quine, "Two Dogmas of Empiricism," in *From a Logical Point of View* (Cambridge, Mass.: Harvard University Press, 1953), p. 22.

2. W. V. Quine, "Meaning in Linguistics," in *From a Logical Point of View*, p. 48.

3. Michael Dummett, *Frege: Philosophy of Language* (London: Duckworth, 1973), p. 473.

4. Ibid., p. 471.

5. Ibid.

6. Ibid., p. 472.

7. Ibid.

8. W. V. Quine, *Word and Object* (Cambridge, Mass.: MIT Press, 1960), p. 119.

9. Ibid., p. 119–20.

10. Dummett, *Frege: Philosophy of Language,* p. 494.

11. Ibid., p. 144.

12. Ibid., p. 490.

13. Ibid., p. 493.

14. Ibid.

15. Ibid.

5

Kinds, Concepts, and Necessity

In Frege's doctrine, a predicate has a referent, and this referent is what he at first called a concept (*Begriff*). Now a concept cannot be the referent of a proper name: it would be an object if it were. But any term to which the predicate "is a concept" was attached would have for its referent an object, and the sentence would therefore be false. That is why he said in "Concept and Object" that "The concept horse is not a concept."[1] But this is not a correct sentence in English, nor is the one it translates a correct sentence in German. The correct expression is of course "the concept *of* a horse" and the concept of a horse is certainly a concept. "The concept horse" is an expression formed by analogy with "the color red," "the god Apollo," "the man Socrates," or "the River Thames": in it "horse" would designate the concept, as "red" does the color, "Apollo" the god, "Socrates" the man, and "Thames" the river. But "horse" in fact signifies a kind of animal; it is this kind of animal, not the concept of the kind, that the word "horse" signifies or means. A concept is some set of descriptions of the kind of thing or some set of propositions about it. The ordinary minimal concept of a horse is that of a four-legged mammal with solid hooves, herbivorous, and used for riding or draught. No description or set of descriptions is synonymous with words like "horse" or "tree" simply because these words are not *descriptions* of the kinds of thing they signify. There are many other descriptions true of horses besides the one I have given and much less familiar, but "horse" is no more synonymous with the set I have given than with much more *recherché* ones, and the reason is that it is not a description of the kind of animal at all. For the same reason it is quite wrong to say that a term like "horse" expresses a concept. Concepts are expressed in sentences, such as "A horse is a four-legged animal, solid-hooved, herbivorous, and used for riding or draught." Expressing a concept and giving a definition can be the same thing.

Those who insist that to recognize or identify anything one must have a concept of the kind of thing regularly fail to say what a concept is, just like Kant. Though they are for the most part *linguistic* transcendentalists nowadays, they accept in effect Kant's distinction between percepts and concepts. Percepts without concepts are the preobjective raw data. One form of this doctrine of concepts is the doctrine that a general term must have criteria of application and that anyone who applies it unfailingly to just the right things must know these criteria of application. It is hard to see how knowing them could be anything but being able to say what they are. A criterion is either that by which we judge that something is so, or the sufficient condition of its being so or such-and-such. To know the criteria of application of a general term would therefore be to know a definition. But we can recognize countless highly specific kinds of things and identify some of them by specific general terms without being able to give more than a vague generic description that applies equally to other kinds of thing. Flowers and plants, birds and insects, are obvious cases in point. We know what various species are like, but when we try to say what they are like we fail to distinguish them from kinds of things that are perceptibly quite different. (Try this with daffodils, earwigs, or phlox.) The doctrine that we must have criteria to identify anything must be, if anything, a thesis in linguistic-transcendental psychology. As for kinds of things with which we are not acquainted, one may know of mangoes and persimmons only that they are kinds of fruit, of argon only that it is a gas, of the nightingale only that it is a bird that sings at night, or of the blackbird only that it is, unlike the ladybird, a bird. These descriptions do not distinguish mangoes or persimmons from other kinds of fruit or from each other, argon from other kinds of gases or elements, or the blackbird from other birds, but if it is said they are inadequate, it must be asked: for what? Adequacy is relative to practical needs and interests. Of many specific kinds of things we have only minimal generic concepts. We distinguish them by the terms, much as people of little classical learning may identify the three most celebrated Greek tragedians just by their different names. We could not readily find out more, however, if we did not know the general terms or names.

It is because general terms are not descriptions of the kinds of things they signify that they can bridge the gaps between what one person and another may know about these kinds of things, how they would describe them, or the concepts they have of them. Thus with quite wide differences of knowledge and experience, each can know what the other is talking about. In an analogous way, a proper name bridges the gap between what one person and another may know about the particular so-named, as it could not do if it had a definite descriptive sense. But the particular so-named is its referent, not what it means. The fact that a particular or individual cannot be identified without identifying the kind of thing it is, does not entail that its proper name has a descriptive sense. Proper names have referents, but most of them mean nothing. The proper names that have a sense are those that have, as Strawson says, grown capitals, like "the Morning Star." This has a sense simply because "morning" means a time of day and "star" a kind of celestial object, though the one in question is in fact a planet.

Many difficulties arise from the notion that some expressions besides proper names and demonstratives always refer or purport to refer to some object, especially those of the type that Russell called definite descriptions. Some of these difficulties led Quine to distinguish contexts in which they are referentially transparent and others in which they are referentially opaque, and Kripke to make his distinction between their use as rigid designators and as nonrigid designators. It is easier just to distinguish those contexts in which they have referents from those contexts in which they do not.

The notion of reference is itself by no means transparent. Is reference a matter of grammar, or of logic, or of the social context— the context of discourse and the intentions of speakers or writers? It seems to be in various ways all three. I take it, in accordance with the facile line of thought, that since "Humility is rare" has exactly the sense of "Few people are humble" and "Few have humility" and since they are one and all contradicted both by "Humility is a virtue that many people have" and by "Nobody is humble," they are logically the same though grammatically different. If we take reference to be a grammatical notion, "humility," the subject term of the first sentence, has a referent, namely humility, and this referent is the subject of the sentence. This would not of course make humility an abstract object—a virtue or disposition is not an object at all. But if the sentence is logically the same as "Few people are humble," where the grammatical subject term is "few people" and the reference indefinite— by contrast with designations like "the British" or "Tom Jones"— then its logical subject is the same. In neither case are we ascribing any characteristic or property to humility, any more than we are if we say "Humility is one virtue that Tom certainly has" (= "Tom at least has humility").

For many expressions, reference depends on discursive context and a wide or narrow community of readers and interlocutors. In one sense of "means," the referent is the one the writer means. Gibbon constantly uses phrases, so-called definite descriptions, like "the conqueror of Gaul" to refer to particular persons who are otherwise identified. We know he means Julius Caesar, that very man, or whoever it happens to be. But the use in detective stories of a similar phrase like "the murderer of John Smith" or simply "the murderer"—"The murderer must have left in a hurry"—before anyone knows who committed the murder, is not like that. Though no doubt only one person is the murderer, he may be any one of several. If "the murderer" referred to the very one, we—or the characters in the story—would already know who it was. Similarly, the noun phrases in "The author of *Sir Gawain and the Green Knight* was the author of *The Pearl*" do not refer to the very person who wrote both works. It is believed that one man wrote both, but we do not know who wrote them, just as in some detective stories it is believed that one man murdered more than one person but we do not know who he was. To know who someone, and especially someone not of our acquaintance, is or was, a proper name is virtually indispensable. Besides that, we need to know where the person is or was located in a social landscape or milieu in relation to other identified people, places, institutions, and things, and for this *other* proper names are indispensable. But we need not be very demanding. Knowing that Aeschylus was an ancient Greek dramatist may count as knowing who Aeschylus was, though the same goes for Sophocles and Euripides. How do people who know no more, know that they were three and not just one? The names are different. That is also the reason "Cicero is Tully" might tell you something or even surprise you, but not "Cicero is Cicero."

Unlike descriptions, proper names have no use but to refer to particular people, places, collectivities, and things, even when they are used in questions like "Who is Trudeau?" by people who do not know to whom they refer. It is obviously important that not too many people in any one milieu have the same proper name. A sentence like "Who is Reagan?" can express as many different questions as there are people called "Reagan." But in a question like "Who is the President of the United States?" the phrase does not refer to the one who is President. It would obviously be just the same question if the actual President had not been President.

"How many planets are there?" and "What is the number of the planets?" express the same question, and "There are nine planets" and "The number of the planets is nine" express the same answer. Likewise, "What color is the book?" and "What is the color of the book?" express the same questions and "The book is red" and "The color of the book is red" the same answer. Likewise, "What does Harry weigh?" and "What is Harry's weight?" and "Harry's weight is 160 pounds" and "Harry weighs 160 pounds." Or again, "What is Mary's age?" and "How old is Mary?" and "Mary's age is 60" and "Mary is 60." Clearly in these contexts, "the number of the planets" does not refer to a number, nor "Harry's weight" to a weight, nor "Mary's age" or "Mary" to a number. The terms that have referents are "the planets," "the book," "Harry," and "Mary."

A person could not understand any sentence if he could not tell whether two ordinary sentences had the same or different senses in a given context and whether they could or could not therefore express the same proposition or question. The first assumption of the facile line of thought is that we all understand our own language in countless contexts, and some of us other languages, too. This being so, we make no bones about saying, in some cases, that the sense is exactly the same, and in others that it amounts to the same.

"The author of *Waverley*" could easily in some contexts be a Gibbonian designation of Sir Walter Scott, but in the sentence made famous by Russell, "Scott is the author of *Waverley*," uttered in reply to the question "Who is the author of *Waverley*?" it is no such thing. The same question is expressed in "Who wrote *Waverley*?" and the same answer in "Scott wrote *Waverley*." Whenever a so-called definite description can be paraphrased in this way, it does not have a referent and does not designate anybody.

IDENTITY OF KIND

Leibniz meant his principle of "the indiscernibility of identicals" to apply only to particulars. But there is a corresponding principle for attributes and kinds. The two principles can be expressed in the following formulae:

$$(I)\ (x)\ (y)\ [(x = y) \rightarrow (\varphi)\ (\varphi x \equiv \varphi y)]$$
$$(II)\ (\varphi)\ (\psi)\ [(\varphi = \psi) \rightarrow (x)\ (\varphi x \equiv \psi x)]$$

If either (I) or (II) were false, a particular could both have and not have one and the same attribute at the same time, or it could both be and not be one and the same kind of thing. The converse of (I) is the principle of the identity of indiscernibles, which can be taken to be true without mishap, but the converse of (II) is certainly false. Though it is a necessary condition for the identity of any attributes φ and ψ that "$(x)(\varphi x \equiv \psi x)$" be true, this is a sufficient condition only for the classes of things that are φ and ψ, not for the identity of the attributes φ and ψ. It hardly needs to be shown that attributes are not classes, or equivalent to classes, but at any rate this shows it.

The so-called criterion of identity for classes is a necessary and sufficient condition: classes are identical *iff* they have the same members. What is the criterion, if any, of identity for attributes? An obvious but wrong answer is that attributes *F* and *G* are identical *iff* "F" and "G" mean the same. Quine expresses something like this view—which is not of course *his* view—thus: "Two open sentences which determine the same class, do not determine the same attribute unless they are analytically equivalent."[2] Quine of course demurs at the notion of attributes—abstract objects in his account—and accordingly does not show that this view is simply false. But indeed it is false. Whereas "*x* has a heart" and "*x* has a liver" determine the same class, if all and only animals that have hearts have livers, but do not determine the same attributes since the heart and the liver are different organs of the body, "*x* has a heart" and "*x* has an organ that pumps blood through the body" determine the same class and the same attribute because the heart and the organ that pumps blood through the body are the same organ. Many other descriptions also uniquely apply to the heart, and when any of them occurs in the context "*x* has an organ that . . . ," we have an open sentence determining the same attribute as "*x* has a heart," since the organ so described is the heart. But none of these sentences has the same sense or expresses the same proposition as any other. "Heart" signifies that type of organ and "the heart" is its common designation when it is referred to or mentioned, but they are not descriptions of it and are therefore not synonymous with any description or set of descriptions of it. They are synonymous only with *cor, coeur, Herz, corazón,* and words for the heart in other languages.

What "heart" means has not changed since it was discovered that the heart pumps blood through the body: "heart" meant the same organ before and after the discovery. There have been many false beliefs about the heart and its functions but, true or false, they were beliefs about the heart. If a concept were the meaning of a term like "heart," if concepts were somehow embodied in such ordinary terms, a language would indeed be a conceptual system or even a theory of the world, as Quine holds, and kinds of things would be concept-relative or, again as Quine puts it, posits of a language. One could be mistaken about what concept a term embodied and what kind of thing it was a concept of, but the kind of thing being concept-relative, one could not have a mistaken, erroneous, or false concept of *that* kind of thing. The kind of thing would change with the concept. If a particular, at first supposed to be one of that kind, proved to have characteristics that conflicted with the concept of the kind, it could not after all be one of that kind, for to revise the concept would be to form the concept of a different kind of thing and to change the meaning of the term.

If *heart* and *cor* did not in most contexts mean the same thing, any attempted translation of an ancient text in which *cor* occurred would be irremediably a mistranslation. *Cor* and many other common Latin words would signify kinds of things very different from those they are usually taken to signify. Translation would be not just difficult, but impossible. Any account of ancient beliefs about and concepts of the heart would be fundamentally misconceived. These beliefs would not be beliefs about the heart but about a different kind of thing that the Romans called *cor,* and since the same would apply to many of the terms in which their beliefs *de corde* were expressed, there would be no way of saying in any modern language what these beliefs were. It would thus be pure illusion to suppose that their writings enabled us to know much more about them than we know about the Etruscans or the Minoans.

"What is the heart?" and "What does 'heart' mean?" are answered and well answered by "The organ that pumps blood through the body," and this may well be the most likely description to occur to anyone now. But many different descriptions might serve to identify the heart, and that is the purpose of "giving the meaning" of such a term. There is an obvious analogy with useful answers to a question like "Who was Cicero?" Kripke speaks of "fixing the referent" both for proper names like "Cicero" and for general terms like "gold" and "meter" by some description or set of descriptions. But this use of "referent" blurs the distinction between proper names and general terms on which he, no less than others, insists. In "Gold is a yellow metal," "gold" refers to gold, but in "I have lost my gold watch," though "gold" still *means* gold—a gold watch is a watch with a case made of gold—it is of course an adjective and it is the whole phrase "my gold watch" which refers. If the type of thing, stuff, or property that a general term signifies or means is called its referent, many people may therefore suppose that there is something else, its meaning or sense, that it has in addition to its referent. There is no such thing. We speak of the sense or meaning of general terms as well as of *what* they mean—the kinds or types of thing they mean—because we think of them as constituents of the sense of spoken and written discourse. Since all words are constituents of the sense of sentences and discourse, they may all be said to have a sense or meaning—"all," "is," "and," and "very" no less than "horse" or "blue." But only general terms mean kinds of things.

There is a class of terms each of which can be uniquely and exhaustively defined or explicated. The minimal concept is also the maximal and a person does not know what the term means at all unless he knows *the* description or has *the* concept. "Bachelors are unmarried men" expresses the concept of a bachelor and gives *the* definition. Besides terms like "bachelor," "sister," "husband" and the like, other terms in this class are "foal," "lamb," "parr," "grilse," "leveret," "pup," and so on. And there are countless technical terms. But terms for natural species like "horse," "sheep," "salmon," "hare," "dog" or "man" are not among them, and one must know what these terms mean by acquaintance or description to know what the terms mean in whose definitions they occur. Terms like "bachelor" and "leveret" as well as many technical terms are *like* expressions introduced in a formal notation as abbreviations of longer ones containing only primitives. We could do without them, as we in fact do without "spinster." But in a natural language the quasi-primitives are just terms that cannot be defined in this way—they are of course definable in the usual way by various useful descriptions. Many of them signify natural kinds.

Given the definition "*x* is a bachelor *iff* *x* is a man and *x* is unmarried," "Bachelors are unmarried" is the logical truth. "If anyone is a man and unmarried, he is unmarried." This is of course a prime example of an analytic sentence. On this model of analyticity, an analytic sentence is either a logical truth or reducible to one with definitions of the extra-logical expressions. The original Kantian notion of analyticity is that in an analytic judgment the concept of the predicate is contained in the concept of the subject. If the concept of a φ is some set of descriptions of a φ, to be contained in the concept is to be one of the set. The complaint to be made about Kant's formulation does not concern the notion of containment but simply his failure to say what a concept is, a failure he has in common with countless later philosophers. The correct concept of a concept covers the concept of a bachelor where there are only two descriptions in the set, and it also covers Kant's example: "Bodies are extended," for whatever other descriptions may belong to the set for bodies, that one does. Another one is certainly "Bodies are composed of matter." But how many others? It seems to depend on how much physics you know. In Kant's doctrine and in many later doctrines, however, analytic judgments, propositions, or sentences are *a priori*. Kant admits an absolute and a relative sense of *a priori*. In the relative sense, what is *a priori* is whatever is assumed, taken for granted, and usually not mentioned in some investigation or inquiry. In the *Prolegomena*, Kant remarks that judgments may be analytic though the concepts are empirical, giving as an example "Gold is a yellow metal." If this is *a priori*, it is so only in the relative sense. It is apparently not in this sense but in the absolute sense that "Bodies are extended" is *a priori*, according to Kant. I see nothing wrong with the use of *a priori* and *a posteriori* in the relative sense—it is the other, absolute sense that I find obscure—but it obviously does not correspond to any distinction between necessary and contingent truths. Kant never seriously attempts to clear this matter up. His main interest was of course the synthetic *a priori*.

In the doctrines I am concerned with there is no such thing as the synthetic *a priori* and they owe rather more to Hume than they do to Kant, though what they issue in is what I call linguistic transcendentalism. The central dogmas of these doctrines are that all necessary truths are analytic and that they are true no matter what—independently of any empirically knowable matter of fact. Besides logical necessity, necessity arises from the meaning of extralogical terms or, as some versions have it, from semantic rules. So with the possible exception of logical necessity, necessity is relative to a language. Necessity is what Quine calls a semantical predicate, and as he says at the end of "Three Grades of Modal Involvement": "Necessity as semantical predicate reflects a non-Aristotelian view of necessity: necessity resides in the way in which we say things, and not in the things we talk about."[3] All necessity is *de dicto,* none *de re.**

Obviously, it adds nothing to the notion of logical truth to call it analytic. The problems of analyticity concern those sentences whose analyticity depends on the meaning or definition of extralogical terms. A central assumption, sometimes explicit and sometimes not, is that the meaning of a general term is a concept, and this is made plausible by the fact that to "give the meaning" is to express a concept, and by the fact that without at least some minimal concept of the kind of thing, we do not know what a general term means. Some philosophers have indeed employed a distinction between what they call conceptual truths and factual truths. Knowledge of conceptual or analytic truths is thus simply knowledge of the meanings of words, a condition of intelligible discourse. To have the wrong concept of φ is therefore the same thing as not to know the meaning of "φ." Even in the great days of this fantastic doctrine, many people observed that concepts changed and concluded that what was analytic at one time might not be analytic at another. But to observe this was only to observe that words changed their meanings.

It is of course true that words acquire new meanings and that some are given rigid and precise definitions for special purposes, especially scientific and technical. It is also true, since no more properties are ascribed to theoretical entities than are required by the theory, that the definition may be coeval with or even, quite often, antecedent to the term. But if the theory is well confirmed and such an entity therefore believed to exist, other properties may be ascribed

---

*That is, *real* necessity and possibility, especially physical necessity, by contrast with logical necessity—necessity *de dicto.*

to it. The atom in the theory of the atomic weights of the elements is not a different thing from the atom in twentieth-century theories of its internal structure. If it were another thing, the theory of atomic weights and the assignment of atomic numbers would either have been abandoned or chemistry would have been cut off from physics. The concept has changed and there have been false concepts of the atom, part and parcel of false theories. But they were concepts of the atom and theories about *it,* not about something else, just as Descartes' concept of the heart as a kind of furnace that heats the blood, is a concept of the heart and not of something else. Conceptual and theoretical problems in science are never problems of language or the meaning of words.

The confusion of the meaning of a general term with a concept rests on the failure to say what a concept is and on the failure to say what "having a meaning" means in the case of general terms. It is not sufficient to observe that general terms do not have the same kind of meaning or are not meaningful or significant in the same way as other kinds of terms—quantifiers, logical connectives, and the like. Everybody knows that. The question is in what way they have a meaning or are significant. The answer, which everybody also knows, is that they have it principally by signifying or meaning various types or kinds of things, properties, relations, activities and so on. General terms are the only terms of which one can ask what it is that they mean, because they alone do mean something—viz., various kinds of things. The answer to such a question expresses a concept, some concept, of the kind of thing. But the concept is not what they mean: the concept of a horse is not the kind of animal that "horse" means. What a general term means cannot be true or false, but a concept of it can.

Since the same thing can commonly be said in different ways, many sets of sentences have the same, or much the same, sense in a context. But terms that mean the same thing, though common enough, are not very common, with the exception of cases like "bachelor" and "unmarried man," where the latter is an explicative definition of the former but not *vice versa.* This and similar examples have led to the further delusion that monolingual lexicography is primarily concerned with synonymy. This mistake is to be found in many philosophical works, but notably in Quine's *From a Logical Point of View.** In

---

*See especially the section entitled "Meaning in Linguistics," pp. 49–50.

"Two Dogmas" one of the two principal themes is treated on this assumption. The notion of analyticity depends on synonymy or sameness of meaning, and it is inevitable that sameness of meaning proves to be just as obscure as meaning. "Meaning is what essence becomes when it is divorced from the object of reference and wedded to the word," says Quine.[4] In fact, the notion of the essence of a kind of thing is that of the set of characteristics that together distinguish it from any other kind. To know what these characteristics are would be to have the essential concept. If the concept is what the word means, as it is in effect in Quine's account, *cor* in Cicero and *cor* and *coeur* in Descartes do not mean the same as "heart."

It is true that we must have at least minimal concepts of kinds of things to understand sentences in which terms that signify these kinds occur. Most examples of analytic sentences express such concepts. These concepts are *a priori,* not in the sense of being non-empirical, but in the sense that we could not know what people were talking about, or say anything intelligible ourselves, if we did not know them. It is with these in mind that people have called analytic sentences trivial or trivially true. Of course this is quite preposterous if you take theorems of logic and mathematics to be analytic.

But more important is the claim that all necessary truths are analytic. "Bachelors are unmarried" is unlike "Bachelors are men" in one important respect, the same respect in which "Racehorses race" is different from "Racehorses are horses." Any bachelor—or almost any—can get married and cease to be a bachelor; that is to say, bachelors are contingently bachelors. But a bachelor cannot cease to be a man or a human being until he ceases to be; that is to say, he is necessarily a human being, the natural kind of being that he is.

One source of the denial, rejection, or simple neglect of modality *de re* is Hume's doctrine that whatever is imaginable or conceivable is possible. Hume, unlike many who have held such a view, has an explicit and fundamental reason for holding it. Our immediate objects are impressions and ideas, and these are mind-dependent: perceptions do not exist unperceived. But, says Hume, "to form the idea of an object, and to form an idea simply is the same thing. . . ."[5] An idea of an object is just an idea. Further, "Whatever we conceive, we conceive to be existent. Any idea we please to form is the idea of a being; and the idea of a being is any idea we please to form."[6] Now all we can ever have when we think of anything is ideas.

Consequently, to ask whether anything could be or happen is just to ask whether the idea of it or of its happening is possible—whether we can have the idea. "Any object may be imagin'd to become entirely inactive, or to be annihilated in a moment; and 'tis an evident principle, that whatever we can imagine is possible."[7] "Anything may produce anything."[8]

The distinction between natural or real possibility and epistemic possibility (conceivability) thus vanishes. Both are conflated with logical possibility, for only that which, in Hume's words, "implies a contradiction" is impossible. Matters of fact, particular and general, are neither logically necessary nor logically impossible. That is to say, they are contingent in *that* sense. This is the sense accepted by many philosophers who might not subscribe to Hume's doctrine of impressions and ideas. According to this view, it is a contingent fact that cows are herbivorous ruminants and not carnivores, and that granite is inedible, as are all facts that we know merely by experience and observation. The problem of induction, as Hume presents it, arises directly from this doctrine that whatever is not logically impossible or implies no contradiction is possible in the only possible sense. The problem is inevitable for the reasons he gives and in his terms absolutely insoluble. But unless one subscribes to some doctrine of impressions and ideas or sense data, one does not have *Hume's* reasons. This may be why so many have thought there must be a way out, or have even doubted whether there is really any such problem. But one cannot accept Hume's assumptions and suppose this.

We can of course be mistaken in thinking that some hypothesis is a law of nature without restriction. But if laws of nature are contingent, any hypothesis that has been true and has indeed been a universal law can cease to be. There would on this account be no certain means of telling on the discovery of an anomaly, conflict, or exception, whether we had been mistaken or not, whether the so-called law had not been a law at all or whether it had been but had ceased to be. Hume's account of why the latter possibility is never seriously entertained, and of why the problem of induction has therefore no practical consequence whatever, is of a piece with his account of why the doctrine of impressions and ideas leaves the belief in the independent existence of bodies quite unaffected. From the doctrine that whatever implies no contradiction is possible, as from the doctrine that what we perceive is mind-dependent perceptions, "we can easily return to our vulgar and natural notions," which in this case are those of natural necessity, impossibility, or contingency. Cows absolutely cannot fly or eat us up; they must ruminate or die. The theorists of the "double existence" (representing and represented, idea and object), as Hume said, on leaving their closets "mingle with the rest of mankind in those exploded opinions"—that the very things we perceive are things that exist independently of our perceiving them. But in doing so, though he does not say this, they likewise mingle with the rest of mankind in the "exploded opinion" that what is *really* possible, necessary, or impossible, is in principle distinct from what we can imagine or conceive.

If laws of nature were not necessarily true, the notions of natural necessity and impossibility would be indistinguishable from those of positive and negative universality. Those who hold that laws of nature are contingently true yet want to speak of physical necessity and impossibility simply fall back into the vulgar and natural notions— "those exploded opinions"—in spite of themselves. The fact that they can't have it both ways can be obscured only by leaving these notions safely in the supposed limbo of "popular discourse." But popular discourse is no limbo. Could a diesel locomotive travel 1,000 terrestrial miles at 30 m.p.h. on one gallon of oil? Absolutely impossible. A diesel engine cannot transform that amount of fuel into sufficient energy. It is impossible in just the same sense as it is impossible for cows to speak Russian, bring forth tigers, or change into weasels. When people say such things are physically impossible, they mean strictly what they say. They do not mean that our concept of a cow is such that if a so-called cow brought forth a tiger or changed into a weasel, we either wouldn't call it a cow any more or change our concept of a cow. They mean that, though you can easily imagine such things happening, no such thing can happen. When one says, for example, that a girl could not have changed into a laurel bush nor a woman into a pillar of salt, one is certainly not saying that the stories of Daphne and Lot's wife cannot easily be understood and imagined—and represented convincingly on the cinema screen. What one is saying is that such things are physically impossible— whether or not one spells it out, for example, by going into the biochemistry respectively of girls and laurel bushes.

Suppose a person, Tom Jones, being of sound mind and not dumb, cannot speak Russian. If he had learned Russian, he could have, and if he sets to work he may yet do so. This is the relative sense of "cannot." Now consider Daisy, a cow. Daisy cannot speak Russian or any other language. But Daisy could not have, nor may she—i.e., nor will she possibly—in the future. The same is true of any other cow. This is the absolute sense of "cannot." It is absolutely impossible that Daisy speak any language. The impossibility is natural or physical.

G. E. Hughes and M. J. Cresswell have it that if we are inclined to say in some important sense "it is impossible for a body to travel faster than light, still this proposition will not count as one which is necessary in our sense; for the reasons which support it consist of facts about the physical universe, and the physical universe might presumably have been other than in fact it is."[9] Now since "necessary" in their sense explicitly means "logically necessary," their point seems to follow simply from the fact that physics is not reducible to logic. But the proposition that the universe might presumably have been other than it is, must mean either that it *might* logically have been other than it is, that its being different would be compatible with the laws of logic—"$E = MC^3$" is not logically impossible—or that it might physically have been other than it is. In view of their use of "presumably," they cannot mean "logically might," for logically, it certainly might. But they cannot without contradiction mean "physically might," since it is physical impossibility they are discussing. The *important* sense in which one may say that it is impossible for a body to travel faster than light is that it is physically impossible—and that means that no body can travel, *could* have travelled, or may yet travel faster than light. But if the physical universe could have been other than it is, as they say it presumably could, then bodies could have travelled faster than light. But the only way to maintain this is to take physical necessity to be relative in the sense I explained before. Tom cannot in fact speak Russian, but he could have and may still. This makes sense because we can say under what conditions he could have—if he had had the opportunity and had taken the trouble to learn it as other people have. But there is no way of thus relativizing physical necessity or impossibility. Under what conditions could the physical universe have been physically different? They would have to be physical conditions and there are no extra-universal physical conditions to appeal to.

C. I. Lewis and other modal logicians have used "conceivable" to explain "possible" and up to a point this is a natural and useful thing to do. Hughes and Cresswell use it to explain the different notions of possibility in their own system T and in Lewis's S4 and S5, and also the concept of accessibility. This gives us a kind of epistemic modality—a state of affairs or world is accessible to another if it is conceivable in that other world given the state of knowledge in that world. But S5, they go on to remark, "reflects on the other hand an 'absolute' sense of the word 'conceivable'—a sense in which to say that a state of affairs is conceivable is to say something about it, without references to the powers of conceiving which may or may not exist in any other state of affairs."[10] Of course we could never speak of any state of affairs if we didn't conceive it, but the idea here is the idea of what is necessary, possible, or impossible whether or not anyone is in a position to conceive it and whether or not there is or was anyone. If no body can travel faster than light, the impossibility in no way depends on what anyone actually conceives or on there being anyone to conceive it. Conceivability is relative and contingent—it depends on there being creatures suitably equipped materially and culturally.

NOTES

1. P. Geach and M. Black, *Frege, Translations* (Oxford: Blackwell, 1960), p. 46.

2. W. V. Quine, "Reference and Modality," in *From a Logical Point of View* (Cambridge, Mass.: Harvard University Press, 1953), p. 157.

3. W. V. Quine, *The Ways of Paradox* (New York: Random House, 1966), p. 174.

4. "Reference and Modality," p. 22.

5. *Treatise,* p. 20.

6. Ibid., p. 66-67.

7. Ibid., p. 250.

8. Ibid., p. 173.

9. G. E. Hughes and M. J. Cresswell, *An Introduction to Modal Logic* (London: Methuen, 1972), p. 23.

10. Ibid., p. 79.

6

Language as Theory

If so-called commonsense realism were a theory, terms signifying various types of macro-object that we perceive, encounter, or manipulate, and also terms signifying the interactions, relations, and properties of such things, would be terms of the theory. In A. J. Ayer's doctrine, such macro-objects are postulated to account for the contents of our sense experiences in a manner analogous to that in which theoretical entities are postulated to account for macro-phenomena in physics. But if, as Quine maintains, there is no conceptual sub-basement of language and we cannot even refer to the contents without mention of the objects, the alleged data having thus to be described indirectly in the terms of the theory, it is not clear what the theory is to account for, or how there could be any test of its truth. The standard notion of a theory is that of a hypothesis or set of hypotheses intended to account for or explain something that is taken to be a matter of fact. In Quine's doctrine, this notion goes by the board: we do not know any facts at all independently of some theory. A theory is just those sentences of a language that we hold true. The theory embodied or presupposed in our experience, perceptual and practical, of such things as people, horses, and trees is then just the language we have learned, all such objects being posits tied to terms of that language. Philosophers who hold this type of doctrine are undaunted by the objection that this is not what is meant by "a theory," that a theory must presuppose some facts, that a language is not a theory but a condition of there being any theory at all about anything, and that many theories are known to be false. Those who contend that facts are theory-dependent seem to regard these objections as question-begging or trivial, for though they grant that there is no conceptual sub-basement of language, they continue to hold that there is a preconceptual, prelinguistic, unobjectified raw material on which different languages impose different structures by positing different objects. Without this assumption, no reason would remain for regarding horses and cows as objects of a theory even in their peculiar sense. And it is on this assumption that the so-called theory of meaning and philosophy of language in the work of philosophers such as Quine and Dummett are based. There is no prior fact of any matter. I quote Dummett:

> What objects we recognize the world as containing depends upon the structure of our language. Our ability to discriminate, within reality, objects of any particular kind results from our having learned to use expressions, names or general terms, with which are [sic] associated a criterion of identity which yields segments of reality of just that shape: we can, in principle, conceive of a language containing names and general terms with which significantly different criteria of identity were associated, and the speakers of such a language would view the world as falling apart into discrete objects in a different way from ourselves . . . for Frege, the world does not come to us articulated in any way; it is we who, by the use of our language (or by grasping the thoughts expressed in that language), impose a structure on it.[1]

> The picture of reality as an amorphous lump, not yet articulated into discrete objects, thus proves to be a correct one, so long as we make the right use of it. . . . Such a picture corrects the naïve conception . . . [which] presupposes that the world presents itself to us already dissected into discrete objects, which we know how to recognize when we encounter them again, in advance of our acquiring any grasp of language at all.[2]

Does he really mean what he seems to mean? Does he really believe it? In effect he denies that there is any such thing as the perceptual recognition of objects, a function which is common to apes, rats, dogs, and countless other animals as well as human infants and which is prior to identification in the sense of naming or applying a general term to something, just as prelinguistic and animal communication is temporally prior to linguistic communication. Without prelinguistic perceptual recognition and highly specialized aural discrimination, no one could ever learn a language or even pick out the sounds of human speech. But according to what Dummett says, a subject could not even pick out human beings, before he picked out the relevant terms and their associated criteria of identity. It also follows from what Dummett says that without a criterion of identity an infant could never learn any word or expression. To know any word or expression is to be able to reidentify it as the same one, but without having learned another expression with its associated criteria of identity, he could never identify any one as the same one. To learn a language, the infant would already have to know one, but unless this one were unlearned, he would also have to know another, and so on ad infinitum.

Whether this doctrine can be fathered on Frege, I do not know. But it certainly goes back at least to Carnap. According to Carnap, the question whether we perceived sense data or whether we perceived something else was not really one of empirical fact but of language. Problems of the primitive data were pseudo-problems. Opposing claims about them, when translated from the material into the formal mode, were sentences about the expressions that occurred as descriptive, primitive symbols; these sentences simply concerned the syntax of different languages. The use of the material mode of speech, said Carnap, led "to a disregard of the relativity to language of philosophical sentences; it is responsible for an erroneous conception of philosophical sentences as absolute."[3] The conception of the claim that we immediately perceive sense data as one of empirical, nonlinguistic fact was erroneous. Likewise the conception of the claim that a thing was a complex of sense data and the claim that a thing was a complex of atoms. In the material mode, as they stand, these claims seem to be incompatible: it is, if anything, the matter of material things that consists of atoms, and a complex of sense data would not be a material thing composed of matter. But what a thing really is, is a pseudo-question, according to Carnap. When transferred to the formal mode, the two theses give merely syntactical sentences concerning different languages: "Every sentence in which a thing description occurs is equipollent to a class of sentences in which no thing designations but sense-data designations occur," and "Every sentence in which a thing designation occurs is equipollent to a sentence in which space-time coordinates and certain descriptive functors (of physics) occur."[4]

The question of what there really is, is neutralized or ruled out of court. The statement that there are no sense data would amount for Carnap to a proposal not to use a sense-datum language or to a statement concerning some language in which the term "sense datum" did not occur. But for a phenomenalist, such as Ayer used to be, since it is a truism that we do in fact perceive sense data if we perceive anything at all, it would amount to a denial that we perceive anything at all. Though we have a choice between the convention for speaking about sense data and the convention for speaking about material things, the existence or occurrence of sense data is not itself a matter of convention: only the use of the term "sense data" to mean sense data is. Thus for Ayer there is a fact of the matter and this fact is not language-relative.

Which side is Quine on? He is on Carnap's side except for one thing; there certainly are stimulations of the nerve endings for Quine, just as for Ayer there certainly are sense data. But for Quine, the phenomenalist's ideas, sense data, or sense contents would then apparently become posits no less than the immemorial and standard posits— middle-sized objects. In his earlier work, Quine regarded horses and trees, electrons and protons, no less than the gods of Homer, as "convenient myths for working a manageable structure into the flux of experience."[5] This flux corresponded to Dummett's "amorphous lump." To substitute stimulations of the nerve endings for the flux, as Quine later does, is certainly to substitute what there is for what there is not. But in the Quinean doctrine, it seems to add just another myth or posit to all the others, for if animals are posits or convenient myths, stimulations of their nerve endings certainly are too.

A classic Humean problem is that we cannot appeal to physical or physiological facts to explain the occurrence of impressions and ideas, since the question is how we could know any such facts, having only impressions and ideas to go on. But according to Quine this fear of circularity is groundless, because "we are confronting a challenge to natural science arising from within natural science."[6] If the question did arise from within natural science, that would not improve matters. But it does not. Though Quine says that "the Humean predicament is the human predicament," by substituting physiological occurrences— stimulations of the sensory receptors—for impressions and ideas or sense data, he has made the Humean problem vanish. But "all we have to go on" has vanished with it. The trouble is not only that the stimulations must be posits by the same token as nerves and organisms, but so must be the terms to which types of stimulation are keyed and without which there are no posits. Everything is a posit and there is nothing to go on. But the whole idea of a posit depends on there being something to go on that is not itself a posit.

"In the old epistemological context," says Quine, "the conscious form had priority, for we were out to justify our knowledge of the external world by rational reconstruction, and that demands awareness. Awareness ceased to be demanded when we gave up trying to justify our knowledge of the external world by rational reconstruction. What to count as observation now can be settled in terms of the stimulation of the sensory receptors, let consciousness fall where it may."[7] Awareness of sense data—or something short of horses and cows—was indeed demanded for rational reconstruction. The trouble was we did not have what was demanded, though many held we did, simply because it was demanded for the purposes of the genetic myth. Why not admit that we do in fact perceive and observe all the variety of things, qualities, properties, relations, and interactions that everybody knows we do? To admit this would be to admit that the bottom had fallen out of empiricist metaphysics.

Its survival really depends on the claim that the problem arises from within natural science, and the project of naturalizing epistemology is really no more than this claim. It is not the project of solving the problem. The problem, as Quine states it, "is that of finding ways, in keeping with natural science, whereby the human animal can have projected this same science from the sensory information that could reach him according to this science. . . . A far cry, this, from old epistemology. Yet it is no gratuitous change of subject matter but an enlightened persistence rather in the original epistemological problem."[8] But clearly this is not a far cry at all from the old epistemology. We just persist in moving into the same old bog. A projection would be a Humean fiction under another name. As for the stimulations, they turn out to be very similar to the Humean images or perceptions.

In his imaginary account of a linguist trying to learn a language without known affinities from a native speaker, the native points towards a rabbit and says "Gavagai." "It is important," says Quine, "to think of what prompts the native's assent to 'Gavagai' as stimulations and not rabbits. . . . In experimentally equating the uses of 'Gavagai' and 'Rabbit' it is stimulations that must be made to match, not animals."[9] But as the following passage shows it is not really stimulations, but either the object or the image on the retina.

> A visual stimulation is perhaps best identified, for present purposes, with the pattern of chromatic irradiation of the eye. To look deep into the subject's head would be inappropriate, even if feasible, for we want to keep clear of his idiosyncratic neural routings or private history of habit formation. We are after his socially inculcated social usage, hence his response to conditions normally subject to social assessment. . . . Ocular irradiation is intersubjectively checked to some degree by society and linguist alike, by making allowance for the speaker's orientation and the relative disposition of objects.[10]

Of course ocular irradiation is not normally checked at all, directly or indirectly, and it can in fact be very different for two people looking at the same object from different angles. The pattern of chromatic irradiation is just the image on the retina under another name. It corresponds to the Humean image or perception. One of the reasons why Berkeley, Hume, and others thought that the perception or image must be two-dimensional was that they thought it must correspond in this respect to the image on the retina.

In *Roots of Reference,* Quine says, "Sensory receptors operate at the level of reception and Gestalt operates at the level of perception."[11] But the image on the retina, which is all his pattern amounts to, has the same Gestalt or structure as an inverted picture of the scene. To take "stimulations" seriously, it is of course absurd to arrest our consideration of them at the nerve endings. But even if we do, we had better forget about the image on the retina and consider what is stimulated and how it is stimulated. The millions of rods and cones are not all the same. Different sets of them react to light of different wavelengths, and their distribution in no way corresponds to the color pattern of the image. There are continual mini-movements of the eye with stops of a tenth of a second, and thus the light from any point of a visibly immobile object falls on many different points of the retina. To speak of a pattern of stimulation is to speak of we know not what. But it is on this that Quine's notion of stimulus meaning depends.

The idea that a picture of the world is projected from the brain—of which the eyes are a kind of outcrop—is an attempt to connect the stimulation of the retina with the things we actually see. For an input of data, there is an output of pictures, projections, or posits in various arrays. We take these posits to be real things, in the primary sense of things that are entirely independent of our perception of them. But no less in Quine's account than in Hume's, we are mistaken in doing so. Quine, unlike Hume, makes reality and truth relative to a language, posits being tied to terms, which are conditioned to sets of stimulations. But on his account what we hear would have to be projected from auditory stimulations just as what we see is projected from visual stimulations, and terms and expressions would of course be posits too. But what terms would they be keyed to?

The question "science asks," according to Quine, is "how it is that people manage from these data to project their story about the external world, true though the story is."[12] On this view, we are inside our own heads; we are our own brains; and what is external is what is outside our heads. What any of us takes to be himself, with a back, front, and sides, is not really him at all, but a posit. He is really a brain, which does not know it is a brain but thinks it is a human being and that the brain is just an organ in his head.

The central assumptions of linguistic transcendentalism, acknowledged or not, are that concepts are embodied in terms and are the meaning of terms, that a language is a conceptual framework or system, and that what there is, according to speakers of a language, is constituted through this framework. Though these assumptions are essential to various metaphysical doctrines, they do not determine which is to be preferred. One position, which is shared by many, is stated by Wilfrid Sellars in the chapter on "Phenomenalism" of his book *Science, Perception and Reality.* It is known as scientific realism.

The familiar world of perceptible things is, in this account, constituted in or through the conceptual framework of Direct Realism, and it is phenomenal in something like the Kantian sense—temporal, spatial, material, causal. The real world, however, is not noumenal and hence unknowable, but the world as construed by scientific theory, and "the assertion that the micro-entities of physical theory really exist goes hand in hand with the assertion that *the macro-entities of the perceptible world do not really exist*" (his italics).[13]

On the face of it, this looks like a version of the popular metaphysical doctrine that the real things are the wee things. This is sometimes ascribed to Democritus, but what he seems to have held was just that big things were composed of wee things, that the wee things—unlike the big things—were indestructible, but not of course that the big things did not exist. It would be self-contradictory to maintain that big things were formed by combinations of wee things but that there were no big things formed by such combinations. Likewise, it is self-contradictory to say that water is H_2O—that any quantity of water is composed of H_2O molecules or that these are the principal constituents of water—but that there is really no water, or to say that there are really no such molecules but only the hydrogen and oxygen atoms, or no atoms but only the subatomic particles. The fact that in ancient atomic theory atoms were conceived as tiny bits of stuff, while in modern theory they are not bits of stuff but constituents of any bit, does not affect the logical point. By the same token, it is absurd to take the opposite road and say that the micro-constituents of gross matter and of bodies composed of gross matter are fictions or do not really exist, but that only the gross matter and the bodies do. Either of these two types of doctrine are incompatible with the notion of matter theory, the theory of the physical constitution of different kinds of matter, which itself leads to no absurdity at all. Neither of them follows from any part of physical theory. They are metaphysical doctrines, as Sellars's use of "phenomenal" suggests.

To make such a doctrine plausible, some ostensibly straightforward, nonmetaphysical reasons have to be given for rejecting what people take for granted, just as phenomenalism requires various ostensibly nonmetaphysical reasons for holding that we do not perceive material things. The only reason of this type which I can find in Sellars for rejecting the assumption that both the big things and the wee things exist, is that "it requires one to say that one and the same thing is both the single logical subject of which an undefined descriptive predicate (e.g., 'red') is true, and a set of logical subjects none of which is characterized by this predicate, thus raising all the logical puzzles of 'emergence.' "[14] In other words, unless everything that is true of the big things is also true of the wee things, there is a difficulty in holding that both exist. There is obviously no such difficulty with macro-constituents of macro-objects. Thus a crowd can stream toward or converge upon an exit, but no person can, and a pyramid can be composed of cubical boxes all of whose sides are vertical or horizontal. But the problem is supposed to arise when the constituents are micro-entities.

Sir Arthur Eddington claimed in the introduction to *The Nature of the Physical World* that "modern physics has by delicate and remorseless logic assured me that my second scientific table is the only one which is really there—wherever 'there' may be." The scientific table is the one which, unlike the familiar visible and tangible table, is "nearly all empty space." "The attempt to melt together Eddington's two tables," says Sellars, "does violence to both and justice to neither."[15] A very different philosopher like Strawson also finds a discrepancy in the assertion that a space is occupied by a smooth green leather table-top and the assertion that what is there is "nothing but a congeries of electric charges widely separated and in rapid motion."[16] We have to recognize what he calls "the relativity of our conceptions of the real" and avoid contradiction by mentioning the different standpoints thus: "This smooth green leather table-top is, *considered scientifically, nothing but. . . .*" But if there were any discrepancy, that would not reduce or remove it. The problem is that the table has a shape, and that it is solid both in the sense contrasted with "liquid" and "gaseous," and in the sense that the materials of which it is made, though they are partly porous and contain tiny pockets of air and other things, are continuous from one surface or edge to another. The congeries of electric charges has none of these characteristics. Clearly, the table cannot be nothing but the congeries of electric charges. And indeed it is not.

The discrepancy is a discrepancy between two pictures. The first is a picture of a familiar table, say a mahogany table with a leather top and brass handles on the drawers; the other is a picture of a very large space with just the odd mote or occasional midge here and there. Of course we cannot blend or "melt together" these two pictures. But both these pictures are macro-pictures as any picture must be. To picture anything is to picture what it is like. We know what some things are like—we have actual experience of them. The only way to picture what anything else is like is to picture it as, in one way or another, like something we know by acquaintance. In the second picture, the subatomic particles figure *as if* they were particles of dust, separated by relatively huge distances. But electrons or protons are not particles in this sense of *bits* of stuff or gross matter. Nor for that matter are atoms or molecules. An H_2O molecule is not a drop or a droplet of water, but every drop, however small, consists of such molecules (mainly!). Though in the second picture the particles figure as if they were bits of stuff, that is not what they are according to the theory—there really should not be anything like that in the picture at all. But however vague the picture, we cannot but picture them as if they were just that. Now empty space, in the ordinary familiar sense, is empty of gross matter or at least of everything but air, and in the case of a vacuum, empty even of that and all other gases. But in electromagnetic theory this notion of empty space plays no role at all. Just as a particle, an electron or a proton, is not a tiny bit of stuff or speck of dust, so the space or region about it is not an empty space but an electric field. The notion of fields of force of various types and the interaction of the forces is essential to the concept of the particles themselves. The picture is irrelevant. A further point is this. The desk is made of different kinds of stuff: the top is of leather, the main structure of wood, and the handles of brass. What happened in the empty-space account to the atoms of copper and zinc and the complex molecules of leather and wood? They are absolutely essential to the account of gross and obvious macro-differences in the stuff of which the desk is made.

Pictures and visual models have their uses and are not to be despised. But though we can imagine the most fantastic things, we imagine them all as macro-things. In the sense in which we know by acquaintance what tables, elephants, and beetles are like, we do not know what atoms are like. We can conceive them but not imagine them. That is where the gap lies. The pictures are on a par, but only one of them is a picture of something we are acquainted with.

To say that perceptible objects do not really exist, says Sellars, is to make a point *about* the framework of Direct Realism, *not in it*, whereas to say that centaurs do not really exist is to make a point *in it*.[17] That perceptible macro-objects do not really exist clearly entails that horses and people do not really exist, since they are perceptible macro-objects. If the proposition that they do not exist makes a point about a conceptual framework, what point is it? If the point is that objects constituted through that framework do not really exist, any statement purporting to be about them would be either false or neither true nor false. But if one asks through what conceptual framework such things as statements, propositions, and sentences are constituted, the answer must of course be the same framework through which macro-objects like people are constituted, since they alone utter sentences, assert propositions, or make statements. If perceptible macro-objects do not really exist, neither do statements or conceptual frameworks. It is easy to say in what conceptual framework the claim is made that to say perceptible macro-objects do not really exist is to make a point about a framework. It is the framework of transcendentalism, according to which things exist only in some conceptual framework. Sellars's account requires two senses of "existence" or "real existence": in the sense in which centaurs do not really exist, people do, but in the sense in which perceptible macro-objects do not really exist, people do not and this sense is the sense required by transcendentalist metaphysics.

In the ordinary sense, what there really is, is contrasted primarily with what people may imagine or suppose there is and, with the exception of things that are obviously people-dependent like language, theories, knowledge, and political institutions, what there really is, is independent of anyone's knowledge, beliefs, concepts, or language. Real things are not in conceptual frameworks. We have concepts of them, which are true or false, and they are true or false because the things are independent of us and of any concepts we have of them.

To say as Sellars does that in his doctrine the macro-object framework is phenomenal in a quasi-Kantian sense is misleading. What is quasi-Kantian is the notion of the conceptual frameworks, both frameworks, through which macro-objects and micro-entities are respectively constituted. In a quasi-Kantian sense both the macro-objects and the micro-objects are phenomenal. There is no ground for saying the one lot are real and the other lot not. Sellars's transcendentalism, which holds that things are constituted through conceptual frameworks, really requires that they have the same ontological status. But Sellars offers what looks like a nonmetaphysical argument for regarding one lot as real and the other lot not.

> To say that the framework (of perceptible macro-objects) is phenomenal in a quasi-Kantian sense . . . is to say that science is making available a more adequate framework of entities which, *in principle,* at least, could serve all the functions, and, in particular, the perceptual functions of the framework we actually employ in everyday life. It is not, of course, to say that there is good reason to put it to this use. Indeed, there are sound methodological reasons for not teaching

ourselves to respond to perceptual situations in terms of constructs in the language of theoretical physics. For while this could, in principle, be done, the scientific quest is not yet over, and even granting that the main outlines are blocked in, the framework of physical objects in space and time, shaped over millennia of social evolution, provides, when accompanied by correct philosophical commentary, a firm base of operations with which to correlate the developing structure of scientific theory, refusing to embrace any stage without reserve as our very way of perceiving the world, not because it wouldn't be a *better* way, but because the better is the enemy of the best.[18]

In this case, as in others, I ask: does he really mean it? And I answer that, of course, he does not really mean it. The obscurity of this passage arises from the transcendentalist doctrine itself. Since entities, macro and micro, are constituted through conceptual frameworks, we ought to be able, if one framework is better or more adequate than another, to substitute the better for the worse, and "embrace it as our very way of perceiving the world." If this framework could in principle serve all "the perceptual functions of the framework we actually employ," then we would actually perceive the theoretical entities. But since there is, as everyone knows, no possibility of perceiving the theoretical entities instead of the macro-objects, "our very way of perceiving the world" must be a gloss on "responding to perceptual situations." A perceptual situation to which we might respond in *either* way, in *either* framework, would then be preobjective, a presentation of sense data or the like. But in case we responded to it in the framework of theoretical physics (of the micro-entities), since we cannot perceive them, as everyone knows, either we should have no perceptible objects at all or we should still have the old ones but just not talk about them nor, since we are in the old framework, about us. The old framework would remain indispensable, since it is through it that perceptible objects are constituted, but we should just never let on that we were using it. Suppose you feel a draft and would naturally ask someone near the window to close it. What do you say in the language of theoretical physics? Now Sellars says that we should not try to do this. But his account of why we should not try is not the obvious one, namely, that we cannot do any such thing and would try in vain. But if the scientific framework is more adequate and better than the old one, *of course* we should. What is better is not the enemy of the best. The worse is the enemy of the best. The better is better.

A close parallel to Sellars's doctrine is provided by those exponents of "cognitive science" who speak of folk psychology. Their assumption, as the word "psychology" suggests, is that folk psychology is a kind of theory, but as the word "folk" suggests, one that from the scientific standpoint has no higher status than folklore. Though some cognitive scientists are none too clear about the distinction between philosophical doctrines of mind and the concepts people actually use in talking about human behavior, the heart of folk psychology appears to be the view that some behavior is intentional and is to be explained by motives (desires, hopes, and fears) and the knowledge and beliefs of the subject. Just as Sellars holds that ordinary descriptions of things and their interactions might be replaced by accounts in the terms of microphysics, so these exponents of cognitive science suppose that some entirely different conceptual system might replace the standard one of motives, reasons, knowledge, and beliefs. But whereas we know in Sellars's case what the replacement concepts would be—concepts of theoretical physics—in the case of cognitive science, we do not know. Since the concepts to be replaced are central to our notion of human beings, human conduct, and human relations as well as to law, history, economics, and much else, even cognitive scientists have sometimes remarked that their abandonment would be, to say the least, disconcerting. But they are surely bound to hold that only according to folk psychology are there people with beliefs and expectations such that they could be disconcerted.

NOTES

1. Michael Dummett, *Frege: Philosophy of Language* (London: Duckworth, 1973), p. 503-504.

2. Ibid., p. 577.

3. Rudolf Carnap, *The Logical Syntax of Language* (London: Routledge, 1937), p. 299.

4. Ibid., p. 301.

5. W. V. Quine, *From a Logical Point of View* (Cambridge, Mass.: Harvard University Press, 1953), p. 44.

6. W. V. Quine, *Roots of Reference* (LaSalle, Ill.: Open Court, 1973), p. 2.

7. W. V. Quine, *Ontological Relativity* (New York: Columbia University Press, 1969), p. 84.

8. Quine, *The Roots of Reference,* pp. 2-3.

9. W. V. Quine, *Word and Object* (Cambridge, Mass.: MIT Press, 1960), p. 31.

10. Ibid.

11. Quine, *The Roots of Reference,* p. 4.

12. Donald Davidson and Jaakko Hintikka, eds., *Words and Objections* (New York: Humanities Press, 1969), p. 294.

13. W. F. Sellars, *Science, Perception and Reality* (London: Routledge, 1963), p. 96.

14. Ibid., p. 98.

15. Ibid.

16. G. F. Macdonald, ed., *Perception and Identity: Essays Presented to A. J. Ayer* (Ithaca, N.Y.: Cornell University Press, 1979), p. 59.

17. Sellars, *Science, Perception and Reality,* p. 97.

18. Ibid.

7

Double Talk

In Hume's account, what any common man calls a hat or shoe or stone is in fact a perception and it is this that he takes to be a real body and to exist when it is not present to him. The identity or spatiotemporal continuity of a so-called body is feigned by the imagination to unite what are really just "broken" but resembling perceptions.

> 'Tis a gross illusion to suppose that our resembling perceptions are numerically the same; and 'tis this illusion, which leads us into the opinion, that these perceptions are uninterrupted and are still existent, even when they are not present to the senses. This is the case with our popular system. And as to our philosophical one, 'tis liable to the same difficulties; and is over-and-above loaded with this absurdity, that it at once denies and establishes the vulgar supposition. Philosophers deny our resembling perceptions to be identically the same, and uninterrupted; and yet have so great a propensity to believe them such, that they arbitrarily invent a new set of perceptions, to which they attribute these qualities.[1]

If what we naturally take to be a real body existing independently of us is such a fiction, it may not be allowed any place in a causal account of the occurrence of our impressions and ideas. Only a real body that was not a fiction would do for that. In all our practical and social concerns we suppose we are dealing with real bodies in this sense. Nature has not left this to our choice. But this is an illusion: bodies are in fact feigned by the imagination.

131

Hume is thus committed to what I call a duplicity thesis, the thesis that anyone who engages in philosophical reflection is condemned to be two-faced and to practice double talk: to talk and act as if his philosophical conclusions were not true. Within the doctrine, our so-called knowledge of matters of fact is founded on the belief in the fictions of the imagination, a belief which rests on "a kind of fallacy and illusion."[2] But this belief itself is the belief that they are not fictions but real things, and the doctrine itself would not be true if people did not act and talk as if they were real things. The philosopher himself cannot but do so, though according to his doctrine they are not. The way out is to recognize that the assumptions of the doctrine are false. But to admit this is to abandon the performance. It is only within the performance that "fiction" in Hume's use has any meaning. We know, and Hume knew and was in a position directly to know, that he wrote the *Treatise*. This is a fact outside the doctrine professed in the *Treatise*. It follows that the doctrine is false and known to be false. The duplicity thesis is required simply to maintain the philosophical delusion.

In Quine's doctrine, material objects are posits of a language or theory. Outside it, they are, as always, real things that exist quite independently of any language or theory. Within the doctrine, truth is relative to a language since true and false statements are about the posits of the language. Outside it, empirical statements are true or false in virtue of the way independently real things are. The philosopher is therefore condemned to act and talk as if the relativist doctrine were not true. But there is worse. According to the doctrine, if it is true, its truth is relative to a language, and does not therefore contradict the usual view of truth which is relative to another language. But if the philosopher claims that his doctrine is true and the usual view false, he can do so, paradoxically, only by assuming that the usual view is true, for the claim can only be sustained by appeal to some fact of the matter which is not language-relative. His claim is therefore self-refuting. Just as the doctrine of the double existence, representing and represented, is, as Hume says, loaded with the absurdity that it at once affirms and denies the vulgar supposition of the independent reality of bodies, any claim that Quine's doctrine is true would both affirm and deny the vulgar notion of truth.

The old epistemology aspired to contain, in a sense, natural science; it would construct it somehow from sense data. Epistemology in its

new setting, conversely, is contained in natural science, as a chapter
of psychology. But the old containment remains valid too, in its way.
We are studying how the human subject of our study posits bodies
and projects his physics from his data, and we appreciate that our
position in the world is just like his. Our very epistemological enter-
prise therefore, and the psychology wherein it is a component chapter, and the whole of natural science—wherein psychology is a component book—all this is our own construction or projection from
stimulations like those we are meting out to our epistemological subject. There is thus reciprocal containment, though containment in
different senses: epistemology in natural science and natural science
in epistemology.[3]

This kind of containment goes back at least to Locke, and neither
he nor Hume made a distinction between epistemology and psychology. Hume had some hopes of showing that the principles of association were "a kind of *attraction,* which in the mental world will
be found to have as extraordinary effects as in the natural and to
shew itself in as many and as various forms."[4] The science of man,
he said in the introduction to the *Treatise,* was "the application of
experimental philosophy to moral subjects." This is entirely similar
to Quine's claim that "epistemology is science self-applied." In its
supposed new setting, none of the problems has disappeared. We
"project our physics from our data." Bodies are posits, not independently existing things that we encounter. But they must be real things
if there are to be any stimulations from which to project our posits.

If they are indeed posits, then the independent reality of things
in our perceptual and practical experience is illusory. If they are
projected from stimulations via terms, they are not independent of
our language and we have no extra-linguistic (perceptual and practical) acquaintance with them. It is just as much an illusion, according to this doctrine, that they exist independently of us and of our
language as it is according to Hume's doctrine: in the one case they
are posits, and in the other fictions, but in neither case are they independently existing real things. Thus it follows from Quine's doctrine
that our prereflective ontological commitment must be the illusion
that posits are not posits, just as in Hume's doctrine the vulgar belief
is the illusion that the fictions are not fictions but real things. The
natural view and the philosophical view cannot be reconciled.

If we take science in this context, as Quine does, to include all our so-called knowledge of the world and things in the world and epistemology to be the doctrine of posits or projections from data, the reciprocal containment view is meant to reconcile them and to make them complementary. But it does not. The split is as radical as ever. Quine says of the reciprocal containment: "This interplay is reminiscent again of the old threat of circularity, but it is all right now we have stopped dreaming of deducing science from sense data."[5] Circularity was no mere threat. How could we appeal to physical or physiological facts to explain the occurrence of impressions and ideas, when we had only impressions and ideas to go on? How could we know any such facts? The problem is not only one of epistemic circularity but of logical incompatibility. If it is true that we project our physics from our data and that macro-objects, like horses, are posits tied to terms of a language, our actual encounters with such things and what we take to be their existence independent of any such encounter are illusory.

"To call a posit a posit," says Quine, "is not to patronize it. A posit can be unavoidable except at the cost of other no less artificial expedients. Everything to which we concede existence is a posit from the standpoint of a description of the theory building process, and simultaneously real from the standpoint of the theory that is being built."[6] This will not even do for neutrinos or quarks and it will certainly not do for horses. There are doubtless many theories about horses, but horses are encountered (browsing, galloping, snorting, etc.), caught, tamed, and ridden. This is a matter of practical experience, not theory. Without such facts there would be no theory. Only a Leibnizian God could be said to concede existence to horses: if anyone somehow failed to recognize their existence, he would be like one of Descartes' madmen.

"Where it makes sense to apply 'true,'" says Quine, "is to a sentence couched in the terms of a given theory and seen from within the theory, complete with its posited reality."[7] From without, from "the standpoint of a description of the theory-building process," it presumably does not make sense to apply "true," but only "true in that theory." A theory in Quine's doctrine is a set of sentences held true, not a hypothesis expressible in different languages. Thus posits are not what are commonly called theoretical entities whose existence and properties are postulated within a theory in the ordinary sense. In this ordinary sense, theories are themselves true or false but not language-relative. But what Quine means by "true" and what he means by "theory" is not just relative to but a central part of his doctrine (or as he would say, "theory").

> Have we now so far lowered our sights as to settle for a relativistic doctrine of truth—rating the statements of each theory as true for that theory, and brooking no higher criticism? Not so. The saving consideration is that we continue to take seriously our own particular aggregate science, our own particular world theory or loose total fabric of quasi-theories, whatever it may be. . . . Within our total evolving doctrine, we can judge truth as earnestly and absolutely as can be, subject to correction, but that goes without saying.[8]

If we take our own theory seriously, that is no saving consideration, for so will anyone else take his. If it makes sense to apply "true" to sentences couched in the terms of any theory, how have we escaped a relativistic doctrine of truth? If we judge truth in our own theory as "earnestly and absolutely" as can be, we will just be deceiving ourselves. We can only do this without deception if we think our theory—or theories in different subjects—is promising and more likely to be true than other theories; only, that is, if it is theories themselves which are true or false and if truth is not theory-relative. What Quine is describing is his own philosophical doctrine in which the concept of truth is changed together with the concept of a theory, and in which truth is theory-relative. But within the terms of this doctrine, he is, in accordance with his own prescription, claiming that it is true "earnestly and absolutely." The doctrine of the reciprocal containment of science and epistemology—or of the natural view and the philosophical view—requires these two concepts of truth. But in fact they are irreconcilable and all that reciprocal containment amounts to is an attempt to have things both ways. From the philosophical standpoint, all objects of any theory are posits and theory-relative, as is truth. But this must apply to Quine's own doctrine or, as he would have it, theory.

In his replies to J. J. C. Smart and Erik Stenius in the volume *Words and Objections,* Quine accepts Smart's opinion that his position is realist, and chides Stenius for failing to realize how this position differs from Russell's. "The burden that Russell placed on sense data, I placed on neural input—adopting thus a black box model with no awareness presumptions."[9] Of course anyone who has read Quine knows this, as Stenius certainly did. But "real" and therefore "realism" are in the same boat as "true." As input to the black box, stimulations are data, though not sense data. But from the epistemological standpoint, if any object like the black box is a posit, so must be the stimulations. It is only in so far as a black box does not regard itself or any other similar black box or any of its posits as a posit that it can take true statements about them earnestly and absolutely to be true. But if it and all its posits are indeed posits, it is entirely deceived in doing so. Quine claims he is able to place the burden formerly borne by sense data on neural input "because of my naturalism, my repudiation of any first philosophy logically prior to science."[10] "Naturalism" in Quine's use raises the same problems as "realism" and for that matter as "true." So indeed does "science." What is prior to science in the usual sense, taking physics, chemistry, and biology to be the core, is practical experience and knowledge of what things are like, how they react, and of what to do with what to get what. But in the traditional way, science or theory is read back into our perception of things (like horses) and our knowledge of obvious facts about them (e.g., that they eat grass). In Quine's doctrine, there are no such things or facts about them prior to science or theory: such things are posits tied to terms of a language and such facts are sentences of that language held true. "Epistemology, for me, is only science self-applied," says Quine, in his reply to Smart.[11] But this is so because his notion of theory or science has been formed in the mold of his empiricist epistemology. A theory, on this view, is not a hypothesis or set of hypotheses to be tested and confirmed or falsified, nor are posits theoretical entities whose existence is established by experimental and practical confirmation of the theory. There are no facts except in the terms of some theory. Horses are posits by the same token as quarks.

There are indeed theories in Quine's sense of "theory," "facts" being theory-relative. One of them is the witchcraft theory of the sixteenth century, which ascribed local misfortunes and disasters to the activity of persons in league with the Devil. For believers, it was not a hypothesis or system of hypotheses to be tested by some kind of evidence against other hypotheses. To accept anything as evidence of witchcraft, one had first to believe in witches, in Old Nick, and of course in God. That is to say, unless one had posited witches and was ontologically committed to witches, nothing would appear to be evidence of their activities. The commitment or belief both excludes the possibility of there being no evidence and prescribes what the evidence is to be. If the evidence was judged sufficient, a person was found guilty of witchcraft as he or she might be found guilty of murder. Within the terms of their theory, witch-hunters doubtless "judged truth as earnestly and absolutely as could be." If it is the case that "we may meaningfully speak of the truth of a sentence only within the terms of some theory or conceptual scheme," in the theory or conceptual scheme of witchcraft "x is a witch" was true for some values of x. Within the terms of the theory, it was just as impossible to doubt that some people were witches as it was to doubt that some people were murderers, though mistaken convictions might occur in the one case as in the other. The theory permitted only such questions as whether a certain person was or was not a witch, not whether the prescribed evidence of witchcraft was evidence of any such thing. In its own terms and with its own ontological commitments, the theory, unlike any genuine hypothesis, did not permit the question whether *it* was true or false. The difference between witchcraft and murder hardly needs to be spelled out. We know that some people have killed other people and that some such cases have constituted murder as defined in law. The only sense in which a person may be said to believe in murder is that he thinks it a good or justifiable way of achieving certain ends. This is not the sense in which a person believes in witchcraft. Murder is no matter of faith or commitment. But witchcraft and the belief in witches is: it is a negative counterpart or complement of belief in good spirits and in God. The pursuit of witch-hunting was only one manifestation, the more commonplace and widespread forms being rituals for protection against its effects.

There being no facts outside the terms of a theory, in Quine's account, any theory must be question-begging in the same way as the witchcraft theory. But Quine's theory is in its own terms a theory. It is in fact the philosophical theory to which his theory actually applies, and it is question-begging in the same way. It permits no question of its own truth. Only within its terms may the philosopher seek truth. To discuss the merits of special theories, we may regress into an overarching theory or language and there find common ground. In Quine's account of semantic ascent, the discussion is carried into a domain "where both parties are better agreed on

the objects (viz., words) and on the main terms concerning them.
. . . The strategy is one of ascending to a common part of two fundamentally disparate conceptual schemes, the better to discuss the
disparate foundations."[12] Since a large part of Quine's philosophy
is embodied in his account of words and the terms in which he discusses
them, however, the fundamentally disparate conceptual schemes lie
as much at the summit as in the foothills.

Quine suggests in *Ontological Relativity* that we should have an
"austere conceptual scheme, free of half-entities, for official scientific
business, and then accommodate the half-entities in a second grade
system."[13] People would obviously be in the second grade system. Any
metaphysics requires an austere scheme for official business, that is,
for performances. But its function is precisely to disconnect the doctrine from science as well as common knowledge and to permit double
talk. The austere conceptual scheme in which Berkeley limned the
ultimate traits of reality had only God, finite spirits, and ideas as its
ultimate objects. But he is on the verge of recognizing this need for
a second grade system when he remarks on the oddity of saying we
eat and drink ideas. We cannot of course think with the learned and
speak with the vulgar as he suggests without failing to say what we
think. All we can do is to expound the austere scheme in our performance. It has no employment; it begins and ends with the exposition.
Later phenomenalists recognized two conceptual schemes, the one of
sense data and sets and series of sense data and the other of enduring
things. But no more than Berkeley did they recognize that the former
cannot be employed or why it cannot. A physicalist metaphysics seems
at first sight to be in better shape. But the admission that the intentional does not reduce[14] is the admission that we and other animals
do not reduce. Reduction would be, among other things, the elimination
of intentional verbs and their replacement by expressions that served
as well but without referential opacity. Since the heart of physicalism
is this reduction or the substitution of physicalist terms to do the indispensable job, the conclusion ought to be that physicalism is wrong,
just as the correct conclusion from the fact that stuff does not reduce
should be that immaterialism is wrong. But in a metaphysical performance it need never be admitted that anything is just wrong, or
that any difficulty is more than a little local difficulty or bubble in
the bag. When the metaphysics is a metaphysics of language, it can
be maintained, as Quine maintains, that there is no fact of the matter,

that is to say, it is only within the terms of some theory or doctrine that anything can be right or wrong, true or false. But it is not a matter of the terms at all. Terms are not concepts. Concepts can be false, since a concept of something is a set of descriptions of it or propositions about it.

Since in Quine's doctrine, a language is a conceptual scheme or system within which there are many subordinate schemes or systems, and a theory is a set of sentences held true, it is not surprising that he discusses his thesis of indeterminacy of translation with reference to a Berkeleyan type of doctrine in *Ontological Relativity,* first as it is held by a deviant Western intellectual and then as it might be incorporated in the natural language of some alien people:

[A] theory might accommodate all rabbit data and yet admit as values of its variables no rabbits or other bodies but only qualities, times, and places. The adherents of that theory, or immaterialists, would have a sentence which, as a whole, had the same stimulus meaning as our sentence "There is a rabbit in the yard"; yet in the quantificational sense of the words they would have to deny that there is a rabbit in the yard or anywhere else. Here, then, *prima facie,* are two senses of existence of rabbits, a common sense and a philosophical sense . . . . [15]

. . . Are there then two senses of existence? Only in a derivative way. For us common men who believe in bodies and prime numbers, the statements "There is a rabbit in the yard" and "There are prime numbers between 10 and 20" are free from double talk. Quantification does them justice. When we come to the immaterialist, and we tell him there is a rabbit in the yard, he will know better than to demur on account of his theory; he will acquiesce on account of a known holophrastic relation of stimulus synonymy between our sentence and some sentence geared to his different universe. In practice he will even stoop to our idiom himself . . . when the theoretical question is not at issue, just as we speak of the sun rising. [That was Berkeley's analogy.—F.C.] Insofar we may say, I grant, that there are for him two senses of existence; but there is no confusion, and the theoretical use is rather to be respected as literal and basic than deplored as a philosophical disorder. . . . [16]

Since the stimulus meaning of an expression or sentence is a pattern of stimulation of the nerve endings and two expressions are stimulus synonymous when they have the same stimulus meaning, only people who "believed in" bodies, nerves, and nerve endings could believe in stimulus meaning. If the immaterialist assented to rabbits on the grounds suggested, he would be guilty of double talk, though in a less glaring way than Berkeley who uses stuff and action terms with abandon, e.g., "When a pin pricks your finger, doth it not rend and divide the fibres of your flesh?" (*First Dialogue,* Philonous speaking)

G.E. Moore remarked that if it were true that some philosophers had been solipsists, it would follow that they were wrong. If it were true that some philosophers were immaterialists, it would also follow that they were wrong. They would have to profess even as they spoke that they had never spoken or written a word, for in the theoretical sense of existence which, according to Quine, is to be respected as literal and basic, their hands and vocal organs would not exist. Immaterialism could only be a doctrine professed in a performance. It is only in a performance that anyone who did not profess immaterialism could admit the possibility that anyone else might be an immaterialist. Quine's immaterialist has one conceptual system for doctrinal purposes and a second grade scheme to accommodate the usual things. But the austere system is professed in doctrinal performances only. The so-called immaterialist may then, like Hume, be merry with his friends.

But the case of the deviant Western intellectual is not the end of this performance:

> [W]hat about the alternative situation where the immaterialist is not a deviant Western intellectual, but a speaker of an unknown language which we are bent on construing? . . . [H]ow could it be determined even in probabilistic terms, that his ontology includes qualities, times, and places, and excludes bodies? I argued in *Word and Object* that such ontological questions regarding a radically alien language make no objective sense. For practical translation we fix on one of the adequate sets of analytical hypotheses, and in the light of it we report even on the native's ontology; but what to report is uniquely determined neither by evidence nor by fact. There is no fact of the matter.[17]

The idea that there is no fact of the matter goes back to the linguistic interpretation of phenomenalism and to Carnap's move from the material to the formal mode, which dispels no problem but inaugurates the metaphysics of language, linguistic transcendentalism. If the question of an immaterialist ontology in a radically alien language makes no objective sense, it is not because there is no fact of the matter; it is only on the assumption that the immaterialist doctrine makes objective sense that it can be held that there is no fact of the matter. Exponents of an immaterialist doctrine—or language, if there were one—would infallibly behave as if they did not believe a word of it. One fact of the matter would be that they were speakers of a language. They could not act out their ontology. There is no way to act it out. There is of course no such language, and Quine never claimed that there was. Why does he use this purely imaginary example to illustrate his thesis of indeterminacy? Linguistic transcendentalism arose out of earlier, mainly empiricist, metaphysical doctrines, and to illustrate it nothing is more natural and easy than to go back to the very doctrine in which more than any other it originated. But we do not need to translate Berkeley's doctrine. That would be ludicrous when he writes so well. All we need do is to spot the false assumptions and claims founded upon them and show that the doctrine is wrong. The same goes for Quine's own doctrine.

When Quine claimed in his essay "On What There Is" that ontological statements followed from all manner of statements of commonplace fact, and that one who regarded an ontological statement as true must regard it as trivially true, it was not because any such statement was indeed true but because some conceptual system made it so. "Judged in another conceptual scheme, an ontological statement which is axiomatic to McX's mind may, with equal immediacy and triviality, be judged false."[18] That an ontological statement follows from some commonplace fact is the essence of many paradigm case arguments. But a commonplace fact in Quine's doctrine is not a true proposition, true in virtue of the way things really are. Appeal to a paradigm case is an appeal not to any kind of thing we encounter and know to exist nor to any characteristic, property, or relation of any such thing, but to the standard sense of terms in some language.

In his contribution to *Words and Objections,* J. J. C. Smart finds "a touch of the paradigm case argument" in Quine's remark in *Word and Object* that we cannot question the reality of physical things because that would deprive words like "real" of "the very denotations to which they mainly owe such sense as they make to us." This is entirely compatible with the doctrine that horses and the like are posits tied to terms of some language, and that it is only according to "the immemorial doctrine of enduring middle-sized objects" that they really do exist. But Quine has got the sense of "real" wrong, as it applies to natural things: what there really is exists quite independently of anyone's recognition of its existence or of his having any term for it or indeed any concept of it. Such is the case with familiar animals like horses. The principal contrast term with "real" in this context is "imaginary." In Quine's doctrine, as in Hume's, this ordinary notion of the independent reality of the things we encounter and know by acquaintance is a delusion and so therefore is the ordinary notion of the truth about them: they are one and all concept-dependent, and true statements about them are true only within some conceptual scheme. But as we noted earlier, this would, according to that doctrine, be true only in the terms of that doctrine.

Quine's only complaint about paradigm case arguments, as he understands them, is that they treat ordinary language as sacrosanct and exalt it "to the exclusion of one of its own traits: its disposition to keep evolving."[19] An innocent might suppose that Quine was appealing here to philology or historical linguistics. One might as well suppose that empiricists appealed to actual perceptual experience and not to what, according to their doctrine, it must be like. No one professing a metaphysical doctrine must ever let it hinge on the way things are or were. The performance would collapse if he did. The ontogenesis of reference and implicitly its phylogenesis as described in *Word and Object* and *Ontological Relativity* are just stories about what might have happened if Quine's metaphysics of language were true. They stand to history, anthropology, and historical linguistics as sacred history stands to history. They are entirely imaginary.

Smart's piece in *Words and Objections* and Quine's reply to it provide a beautiful example of a metaphysical *pas de deux,* in which each excels himself under the inspiration of the other. Smart offers the following argument for the claim that there might turn out to be no physical objects. Two people could call one set of manifestations respectively a case of epilepsy and a case of demonic possession. But the expression "demonic possession" being theory-laden and the theory being false, there is no such thing as demonic possession. "Surely, therefore," says Smart, "there might turn out to be no physical objects of the sort to which Dr. Johnson referred. . . ."[20] He goes on to quote Quine with approval as follows: "One could even end up, though we ourselves shall not, by finding that the smoothest and most adequate overall account of the world does not after all accord existence to ordinary physical things."[21] Quine takes this to be the suggestion that "existence in a theory-laden sense could intelligibly be denied of visible and tangible objects," and says, "This is very much my view."[22] He suggests that in a superstitious community one might learn "demonic possession" holophrastically as an observation term applied to epileptic fits as paradigm cases. Then, learning the theory of demons and possession by demons and that it is false, "one could warp the term away from the paradigm cases that originally gave it what meaning it had for him. So it is with 'there is.' "[23] To warp the term away from epileptic seizures would be to apply it to something else. But why would anyone do that? There is a familiar set of terms still applied descriptively to people—"sanguine," "phlegmatic," "choleric," and "melancholic." We can learn the theory of the humors and that it is false. But why should we warp these terms away from the kinds of cases they apply to and start applying them to other kinds of cases? However it is with "there is," "demonic possession" will not cast any light on it. So how is it with "there is"?

> Growing up in a community of believers in stones and rabbits we first learn "there is" in connection with stony and rabbity sorts of stimulation. Eventually, after mastering the logic of quantifiers or their vernacular equivalents, we invest "there is" with a theoretical quality and are prepared, in an extremity, to warp it away from its paradigm cases. This is why I have urged the inscrutability of reference; existence in its final state is theoretical. For convenient communication between persons with unlike ontologies there arises, even, a double usage: the sophisticate who has dismissed rabbits or perhaps numbers as values of variables will still assent to "There are rabbits" and "There are large prime numbers" holophrastically, while reserving the right to paraphrase if anyone wants to make ontological capital of the internal constitution of these sentences.[24]

Quine's notion of holophrastic assent depends on that of stimulus meaning, but even if that notion were any good, nobody would actually know what the pattern of stimulation of the nerve endings was. There are no such things as rabbity or stony sorts of stimulations of the nerve endings. If a person assented to "There are rabbits," he would have to assent to "That's a rabbit" or "There's a rabbit" when he saw a rabbit in plain view. Warping "there is" away from this paradigm case, however, and taking "existence" or "there is" in its final state to be theoretical, the sophisticate would have to assent in the presence of visible tangible rabbits to "There are really no such things as these rabbits there." If he were not well understood to be a metaphysician giving one of his perfectly harmless performances, he might be taken for one of Descartes' madmen.

Let us leave aside the idea that we believe in stones and rabbits as some believe in gods, demons, fairies, and Santa Claus, and consider the idea that we first learn the existential use of "there is" and "there are" in connection with things like stones or rabbits. Since there is no occasion to say there are stones or rabbits—but only to say *"There's* a stone" or *"There's* a rabbit"*—this seems a little unlikely. The likely thing is that we first learn "there are" in contrast with "there are no . . ." and we first learn this in connection with things like gods, fairies, ghosts, and Santa Claus. Not only are there no fairies at the bottom of our garden or anywhere else in the garden, there are no fairies anywhere at all, hence, more succinctly, there are no fairies. Except in contrast to such imaginary things as these, who would ever think of saying there are rabbits or stones? A well-known example of "there is no . . ." occurs in Psalm 14: "The fool hath said in his heart there is no God." But it is hard to find any example of "there is." The example in the Oxford English Dictionary is from Evelyn concerning Epicurus's *denial* that there is a God. "There is no . . ." and "There are no . . ." require not only the notion that some stories are false or fictitious but also the notion that the beings they are ostensibly about are fictitious. To learn "there is no . . ." is in effect to learn the distinction of real and imaginary. There are of course fictitious or imaginary beings, but there are not two kinds of beings, real and imaginary. Imaginary beings are not beings but fictions. The gryphon is an imaginary animal, and also an heraldic animal, but it is not an animal.

If there is any warp in the use of "there is," it does not arise from these distinctions but with metaphysical doctrines and especially with those in which skepticism and phenomenalism have played a fundamental role. Thus in "Two Dogmas of Empiricism," material objects figure as "myths for working a manageable structure into the flux of experience." The unrecognized myth here is that of the flux of experience.

The nearest thing to a fact known by observation in Quine's doctrine is an observation sentence or *Protokollsatz*. But it is the sentence that matters, not the observation or what is observed, and the doctrine disregards some obvious facts about observation or perception. If there are no pretheoretical facts, there are of course none regarding observation or perception. In Quine's version, "a sentence is an observation sentence if all verdicts on it depend on present sensory stimulation and no stored information beyond what goes into understanding the sentence . . ." and if it is a sentence "on which all speakers of the language give the same verdict when given the same concurrent stimulation."[25] Suppose we ask whether the "k" sound in "keel" and "call" is the same. The answer seems to depend on nothing but understanding the question and hearing the sounds. When asked this question, some people say the sounds are the same and some say they are different. But those who say they are the same, when asked to listen again, usually agree that they are different. Even though all were agreed in the end, however, their replies would not count as observation sentences since not everyone gives the same reply every time. Now this example illustrates the commonplace fact about perception that we have to look or listen carefully to catch or spot some things. Sometimes we do and sometimes we don't. Perception is selective both spontaneously and deliberately. In many kinds of perception what is needed is practice, just as it is needed in the development of motor and manual skills. Quine's notion of the observation sentence is useless because the notion of observation on which it is ostensibly based is a mere ghost—there is really no notion of observation there at all but only stimulations of the nerve endings, and sentences. Russell Hanson, Quine remarks, "ventured even to discredit the idea of observation, arguing that so-called observations vary from observer to observer with the amount of knowledge they bring with them."[26] The point requires no argument as regards real observation; it would discredit only the Quinean ghost. We must know what to look for to spot many things. In experiments we have to look for what should be observable according to the theory, not any of the countless other things that any casual bystander might observe.

When a theory is well established we may speak of what we observe in the terms of the theory—of a discharge of electrons, for example, instead of a flash, because according to the theory the flash is a discharge of electrons. But what some philosophers mean by "a theory-laden observation" is that the terms of the theory determine what we actually perceive. This claim is constantly assumed by many people without the slightest effort to justify it or to give precise examples. It is an offshoot of metaphysical doctrines of science in the classic empiricist mold, according to which uninstructed perception of things itself embodies the so-called commonsense theory. A person ignorant of a theory can in fact be told what to watch for and can see it in entire ignorance of its significance, and what he sees will be just what the theorist sees. Observation is of course theory-*guided,* but unless what is observed is independent of the theory, there is nothing for the theory to account for or explain and no way of testing it.

NOTES

1. *Treatise,* p. 217.
2. Ibid., p. 189.
3. W. V. Quine, *Ontological Relativity* (New York: Columbia University Press, 1969), p. 83.
4. *Treatise,* pp. 12–13.
5. Quine, *Ontological Relativity,* pp. 83–84.
6. W. V. Quine, *Word and Object* (Cambridge, Mass.: MIT Press, 1960), p. 22.
7. Ibid., p. 24.
8. Ibid.
9. Donald Davidson and Jaakko Hintikka, eds., *Words and Objections* (New York: Humanities Press, 1969), p. 298.
10. Ibid.
11. Ibid., p. 293.
12. Quine, *Word and Object,* p. 272.
13. Quine, *Ontological Relativity,* p. 24.
14. Quine, *Word and Oject,* pp. 221–22.
15. Quine, *Ontological Relativity,* p. 98.
16. Ibid., p. 99.
17. Ibid., p. 103.
18. W. V. Quine, *From a Logical Point of View* (Cambridge, Mass.: Harvard University Press, 1953), p. 10.
19. Quine, *Word and Object,* p. 3.
20. Davidson and Hintikka, *Words and Objections,* p. 8.
21. Quine, *Word and Object,* p. 4.
22. Davidson and Hintikka, *Words and Objections,* p. 293.
23. Ibid.

24. Ibid.
25. Quine, *Ontological Relativity,* pp. 86–87.
26. Ibid., p. 87.

8

Metaphysical Translation

Quine's idea of radical translation and his thesis of indeterminacy of translation are corollaries of his linguistic transcendentalism. The first task of his imaginary linguist, who is to construct a grammar and a lexicon of a language without known affinities, is to establish the stimulus synonymy of some expressions in his own and the other language. When the heathen informant says "gavagai" in the presence of a rabbit, the question is not whether he is referring to the rabbit, far less whether "gavagai" means the same as "rabbit," but whether "gavagai" is stimulus synonymous with "rabbit" or with "rabbit parts," "rabbit stages," or "rabbithood." It is stimulations that must be made to match, not animals or other things. If the linguist took "rabbithood" to be a well-formed English word, as many philosophers have taken "thinghood" and "eventhood" to be in their performances, his case would be hopeless. By "rabbit stages" Quine seems to have in mind something like segments of a four-dimensional object or world line. Even when the options are narrowed down to "rabbit" and "rabbit parts," the example is, as Quine says, contrived and perverse and a linguist would have no patience with it.[1] But the doctrine permits only contrived and perverse examples.

The fundamental concept is that of an object: an object is a posit of a language, and to be is to be an object or value of an individual variable. But all translation depends ultimately on radical translation, and radical translation on the equation of some few sentences that have the same stimulus meaning—a pattern of stimulation of the nerve endings. "Sentences translatable outright, trans-

148

latable by independent evidence of stimulatory occasions, are sparse and must woefully underdetermine the analytical hypotheses on which the translation of all further sentences depends."[2] Different systems of analytical hypotheses may specify "mutually incompatible translations of countless sentences insusceptible of independent control." Two incompatible sentences of language *A* may therefore both be translations of a true sentence in language *B*, and one or both of them may be false.

> There is an obstacle to offering an actual example of two such rival systems of analytical hypotheses. Known languages are known through unique systems of analytical hypotheses established in tradition or painfully arrived at by unique skilled linguists. To devise a contrasting system would require an entire duplicate enterprise of translation, unaided even by the usual hints from interpreters. Yet one has only to reflect on the nature of possible data and methods to appreciate the indeterminacy. . . .[3]

An analytical hypothesis is not the hypothesis that in a certain type of context two terms or expressions mean the same kind of thing. The primary equations on which all others are based are equations not of meaning but of stimulus meaning—the stimuli being not things in view or in reach, but stimulations of the nerve endings. Since no linguist has ever worked with that notion, and a linguist would get nowhere if he tried, it follows that no known language is known through any such thing. In his reply to Erik Stenius in *Words and Objections*, Quine says that the reading of chapter 2 of *Word and Object* as instructions for field linguists is "an embarrassing misinterpretation." But he sticks to the position that "ocular irradiation is intersubjectively checked to some degree by society and linguist alike." In fact, it is not, and linguists make no conjectures about irradiation patterns on their interlocutors' retinae. Nor do they regard themselves or their informants or other animals and things as posits. The obstacle to offering two rival systems of analytical hypotheses is that there is not even one. The embarrassment arises not from any misinterpretation but just from taking the metaphysical doctrine literally as a factual thesis. It is similar to a professed immaterialist's embarrassment at the conclusions that follow from taking his doctrine that there is no matter as a factual thesis.

It is not surprising that some people have failed to understand

Quine's thesis of indeterminacy and how it follows—as it does—from his assumptions. But in the section devoted to causes of "failure to perceive the indeterminacy," as the word "perceive" clearly shows, Quine makes no distinction between understanding his thesis and perceiving its truth. The supposed causes of the failure miss the real, factual objections to the whole doctrine.

> A fourth and major cause of failure to appreciate the point is a stubborn feeling that a true bilingual surely is in a position to make uniquely right correlations of sentences generally between his languages. This feeling is fostered by an uncritical mentalistic theory of ideas: each sentence and its admissible translations express an identical idea in the bilingual's mind. The feeling can also survive rejection of the ideas: one can protest still that the sentence and its translations all correspond to some identical even though unknown neural condition in the bilingual. Now let us grant that; it is only to say that the bilingual has his own private semantic correlation—in effect his private implicit system of analytical hypotheses—and that it is somehow in his nerves. My point remains; for my point is then that another bilingual could have semantic correlations incompatible with the first bilingual's without deviating from the first bilingual in his speech dispositions within either language, except in his dispositions to translate.[4]

A bilingual with any experience in translating knows that there is sometimes not only a good translation but more than one, but equally he knows that in other cases there is no good one and sometimes none at all. If he did not understand the sense of what a speaker or writer says in its context, he could not of course know any such thing. The notion of understanding what a person says, asks, orders, requests, etc., as in fact we regularly do, far from being fostered by the metaphysical doctrine of ideas in the mind, is directly opposed to it. What a person says is public, he says it out loud, and we hear what he says as we see what he otherwise does. The sense of it is no more hidden in the one case than in the other, and neither more nor less liable to misunderstanding. The idea of an identical neural condition corresponding to sentences in different languages would only occur to anyone who held Quine's own view that the infinite set of sentences of a language corresponds to an infinite set of neural mechanisms.

If the doctrine of indeterminacy of translation were a factual, testable thesis, there would have to be cases in actual languages where it might be claimed the indeterminacy showed up, in spite of Quine's fanciful historical explanation of why it is not likely to show up. An immaterialist language, being patently imaginary, will not do as a real case in point. In *Ontological Relativity*[5] Quine attempts to provide three genuine cases in point. But they turn out to depend on his own metaphysical doctrine, incorporated not in English but in his parsing of English.

The first case concerns expressions containing classifiers in Japanese, of which, according to Quine, two different accounts can be given in English. In one account, the classifier attaches to a numeral before a general term; in the other it attaches to the term that follows the numeral. In his example, the translation from Japanese in the former case would be "five oxen" and in the latter case "five head of cattle." For his purpose, Quine stipulates that "cattle" is a term covering only bovines and that "ox" applies to each and every bovine. Inscrutability of reference, says Quine, "is thus illustrated by a point of practical translation."

It is hard to see how either the meaning or the reference can be obscure, far less inscrutable. Such is the facile line of thought. Whether the classifier goes with the numeral or with the term seems to be like the question whether in the sentence "He went out to the balcony," "out" is an adverb or part of a compound preposition "out to" in the adverbial phrase "out to the balcony." A French speaker appealing to "he went out" as the translation of "il sortit" might be inclined to say it was an adverb, though this would be wrong in the case of "He went out of the room" (cf. "into the room"). But the sense would be unaffected by the parsing. So it seems to be in Quine's example. But Quine's point depends on his peculiar parsing, not of Japanese, but of English. He takes "cattle" to be what he calls a mass term, and "five head of cattle" to be analogous to "five sticks of wood." "Cattle," however, is not a stuff term like "wood" but a collective term like "people." Though "cattle" is not a count noun, cattle, like people, can be counted. One hardly needs "head of"—one can very well say "five cattle" just as one says "five people" but not of course "five wood." It happens in this case that the plural verb shows that "cattle" is plural, not singular like "wood." But compare "le bétail" (cattle) in French. It is of course singular, and one must say either "cinq têtes de bétail" (five head of cattle) or "cinq bêtes" (five animals). But it is also a collective noun signifying a plurality of animals. One can count (*compter, dénombrer*) *le bétail.* "Les bestiaux" is also a collective noun, synonymous with "le bétail," but plural like "les gens" (people). Unlike "cattle" and "people" these cannot be qualified by numerals: "five people" is "cinq personnes." There is no obscurity of meaning or reference here. But Quine, parsing collective terms as stuff terms, would have to say there was, as in his example from Japanese.

The other examples Quine attempts to give of inscrutability of reference depend on his distinction between concrete general terms and abstract singular terms; on his doctrine that singular terms refer to single objects, abstract or concrete; and his failure to acknowledge that general terms signify types or kinds of things, properties, relations, etc. "Green," he says, is a concrete general term in "The grass is green," but it is an abstract singular term, naming an abstract object, in "Green is a color."[6] But since green is a color, "green," whether adjective or noun, is always a general term signifying that color. To say that green is the color of the grass is therefore just to say the grass is green or that it has that color, viz., green.

The remaining example depends on the same doctrine. Quine contrasts "Alpha is a letter" with "This inscription begins with an alpha," and maintains that "the objects referred to by the word are very different under the two uses; under the one use the word is true of many concrete objects, and under the other use it names a single abstract object." Hence we have "systematic ambiguity."[7] But there is no ambiguity in these examples. The genuine distinction is between type and token, or sort and particular. There can be type-token ambiguity as in "This is my favorite flower," where a speaker may mean either one particular flower or the species or variety. But in Quine's example there is no such ambiguity. When we write alpha and when we write an alpha on the blackboard we do one and the same thing. To write two alphas is to write alpha twice. Speaking of stimulus meaning, Quine says that the stimulation is "a universal, a repeatable event form." He goes on: "We are to say not that two like stimulations have occurred, but that the same stimulation has recurred."[8] Two like stimulations would be two of one type, the first an occurrence of it and the second a recurrence of it. Of course Quine knows this, but in his performance he must not let on.

Regarding the two uses of "green" and "alpha," Quine says:

We can of course tell the two uses apart by seeing how the word turns up in sentences: whether it takes an indefinite article, whether it takes a plural ending, whether it stands as a singular subject, whether it stands as a modifier, as predicate complement, and so on. But these criteria appeal to our special English grammatical constructions and particles, our special English apparatus of individuation, which, I have already urged, is itself subject to indeterminacy of translation. So, from the point of view of translation into a remote language, the distinction between a concrete general and an abstract singular term is in the same predicament as the distinction between "rabbit," "rabbit part," and "rabbit stage." Here then is another example of inscrutability of reference, since the difference between the concrete general and the abstract singular is a difference in the objects referred to.[9]

The entire point hinges on his own metaphysical parsing of English, and vanishes without it.

The imaginary linguist not only reads his "ontological point of view" into the Heathen language, he projects his conceptual system or theory of reality upon the other. But some sentences to which Heathens universally assent and which are therefore stimulus-analytic in Heathen are translated by sentences that are not only not stimulus-analytic in English, but in most opinions false. Quine's imaginary example is "All rabbits are men reincarnate." This, he says, is translator's license, "a bold departure to be adopted only if its avoidance would seem to call for much more complicated, analytical hypotheses. For certainly the more absurd or exotic the beliefs imputed to a people, the more suspicious we are entitled to be of the translations; the myth of the prelogical people marks only the extreme. For translation theory, banal messages are the breath of life."[10]

In his reply to Chomsky in *Words and Objections*, Quine makes a similar remark concerning the attribution of absurd beliefs to himself: "The more absurd the doctrine attributed to someone, *ceteris paribus*, the less the likelihood that we have well construed his words."[11] But as Cicero justly observed: "Nihil tam absurdum dici potest quod non dicatur ab aliquo philosophorum" (Nothing so absurd can be said that is not said by some philosopher) (De Divin. II, lviii). Exotic beliefs are just the less familiar ones. Of course nobody wants to be taken for an *insensé*. Thus neither Berkeley nor any other immaterialist wants to say there are no such things as food and drink. Nor doubtless will anyone who holds that "beauty" or "humility" names abstract objects want to say that "Mary has beauty" entails "Mary has an abstract object" or that if it is true, Mary has something that she would not have if she were merely beautiful. However, if the doctrines were factual theses, these things would follow. If their authors affirmed the doctrines but denied the consequences, they would lend some credence to the myth, if not of prelogical peoples, at least of prelogical individuals, to wit, some philosophers. In their metaphysical performances therefore, these consequences must not be allowed to follow. To avoid this, the only thing they can do is to maintain that we have not well construed their words or, more elaborately, that they are employing a language in which no such things follow. If in spite of the fact that they are using the same natural language, we grant this notion of a language, then to say we have misconstrued their words will be to say that we have mistranslated them.

Let us apply the thesis to Missionary or Quinese and to the facile Heathen line of thought in the case of "alpha" in Missionary and "alpha" in Heathen. Though the stimulus meaning is doubtless the same, we cannot determine whether the referents of "alpha" in Missionary and "alpha" in Heathen are the same. Reference is inscrutable. If a Missionary like Quine and a Heathen like me each equates "alpha" in his own language with "alpha" in the other's, each of us will already have read his ontological point of view into the other's language. He will take a Heathen like me to be speaking of an abstract object and I will take a Missionary like him to be speaking of this Greek letter here, α, which is called "alpha." There being no fact of this or any other matter, except in the terms of some theory, and theories being language relative, there is no question of one concept being the right one, nor of whether each of our translations of "alpha" in the other's language as "alpha" in our own is correct. It makes no difference that we are both bilingual in Missionary and in Heathen.

> It makes no real difference that the linguist will turn bilingual and come to think as the natives do—whatever that means. For the arbitrariness of reading our objectivations into the Heathen speech, reflects not so much the inscrutability of the native mind as that there is nothing to scrute.[12]

Just as, according to Quine, a speaker of another language, Immaterialism, might utter the Heathen sentence "There's a rabbit" and point to a rabbit when conversing with Heathen shooting companions, so Quine might say "Alpha is the first letter of the Greek alphabet" and point to a letter with the words, "That's it there," when conversing with Heathen beginners in Greek, though in Missionary only an alpha could be there, and alpha is quite a different object.

The facile Heathen line of thought is just that Missionary is a conceptual system and doctrine, but not a language. Nor is any language a conceptual system or doctrine. But the concept of a language in the Missionary doctrine is projected on what are in fact languages and they are therefore taken to be conceptual systems or doctrines. Since each of us, Quine and I, have both concepts of alpha, we both know the two concepts of alpha are not the same. But we know that the referent of "alpha" is the same, viz., the Greek letter α. Reference is not inscrutable. But the referent being the same, at least one of the two concepts must be false, and there is no doubt which one that is. Alpha can be written down as often as you please and is to be found *passim* on any page of Greek. But an abstract object cannot be and is nowhere to be found. Alpha is therefore not an abstract object, just as a duck is not a mammal and chalk is not cheese.

Just as the concept of alpha in Quine's doctrine is the wrong concept, so is the concept of a language and so is this concept of bilingualism. Terms are not concepts, reference is not concept-relative, and concepts and truth are not language-relative. A bilingual's concepts, knowledge, theories, and beliefs are not tied to one or to the other of his languages. Understanding what a person says in any language and thus knowing what he thinks is quite distinct from thinking as he does. Terms in one language may, and often do, have no translation in another, nor, consequently, sentences containing these terms. But there is usually no difficulty in expressing concepts of the kinds of things they signify, if there is any such concept. The difficulty, when it arises, lies in the concepts themselves. For some terms there is just no clear concept of what they signify, though they ostensibly signify something. "God," "the Mind" and "the Self" are such terms. There are many such terms in many languages. Many bumble words have uses to which any clear concept of what they mean would be inimical. A philosopher like Derrida floats on a sea of them. Quine, in comparison, is an angel of lucidity. But he is bad enough. Like his imaginary immaterialist, he has two conceptual schemes or systems, one for rigorous doctrinal purposes and the other for daily conversation, the facile Heathen line of thought. Not surprisingly, it is sometimes difficult to know which he is employing. The lines get crossed, or perhaps we have what in his terms would be impromptu, unannounced translations from one language into the other. Thus when he speaks of exotic beliefs, a belief might seem to be a proposition believed. But in that case, a translation of a sentence expressing it in one language would be a sentence expressing it in the other. A bilingual who translated it into another language could not conceivably both believe and not believe it. According to Quine's strict doctrine, however, there is no such determinable same thing expressed in two different sentences of the same or different languages and translation is always relative to some set of many possible sets of analytical hypotheses. Beliefs are therefore relative to languages. This concept of a belief—like everything else in the doctrine—is itself therefore relative to a language. Any claim that the doctrine is true and Heathenism false is a lapse into Heathenism: whether it is made in Missionary or in Heathen it is self-refuting. It is not surprising that Quine seems unable to distinguish a failure to understand his doctrine from a claim that it is false.

A Heathen philosopher can hardly call the Missionary doctrine exotic. It is right in the mainstream. Regarding its central notion of abstract objects, it is perhaps worth noting that the original doctrine of supratemporal, nonspatial particulars was advanced by the philosopher who in the *Phaedo* also advanced a doctrine of reincarnation, though of souls, not of men, and though he never mentioned rabbits.

NOTES

1. W. V. Quine, *Ontological Relativity* (New York: Columbia University Press, 1969), p. 34.
2. W. V. Quine, *Word and Object* (Cambridge, Mass.: MIT Press, 1960), p. 72.
3. Ibid.
4. Ibid., p. 74.
5. Quine, *Ontological Relativity*, p. 35 ff.
6. Ibid., p. 38.
7. Ibid.
8. Quine, *Word and Object*, p. 34.

9. Quine, *Ontological Relativity*, p. 39.

10. Quine, *Word and Object*, p. 69.

11. Donald Davidson and Jaakko Hintikka, *Words and Objections* (New York: Humanities Press, 1969), p. 34.

12. Quine, *Ontological Relativity*, p. 5.

9

Reasons and Motives

If we take states to contrast with actions, activities, events, and processes, then dispositions are one kind of state. But not all states are dispositions. In the case of human beings, widowhood counts as a state, but it is not a disposition to do any specific thing or range of specific things or to act in any particular fashion. Many states manifested in behavior are not dispositions. In particular, factual knowledge and beliefs are not dispositions to act in any way at all. They inform action or, in other words, people act in the light of their knowledge and beliefs, and in countless cases would doubtless act otherwise if they knew more or had different beliefs. Thus a person goes to the cinema in the knowledge that a certain film is on and would not go unless he knew or believed this; but the knowledge or belief is not a disposition to do this or to do anything, as a liking for a certain type of film or a desire to see this one would be. Such a liking or desire is a disposition of a special type—it is a motive. What one knows or believes may provide reasons for acting in one way rather than another, but it does not provide or constitute motives. Thus knowledge of the height and steepness of an obstacle in relation to its breadth may be a reason for going round it, but only if one has a motive for getting to the other side and none, or a less urgent one, for getting to the top or staying put. Motives are often called reasons, but reasons for acting in one way or another are always subordinate to motives. Motives are always motives to act, whether one acts on them or not, and the motive or motives of or for an action are what one desires, hopes, or expects to be the result. What one knows or believes is never a motive; nor is it any other type of disposition. Abilities and skills are also states but not dispositions. Though various manual and other dispositions or habits go into them, none of these is a disposition to do any of the things in which the ability or skill is displayed or for which it is required. In the case of one's native language, knowing it is the ability to speak and understand it and to say whatever one pleases in it. But it is not a disposition or set of dispositions to speak, far less to say anything or utter any sentence on any occasion.

Now the notion of a disposition, as Quine employs it, is the one which is relevant to S-R (stimulus-response) theory. Whether they are innate or the result of conditioning, dispositions are dispositions to behave in specific ways under specific types of stimulation and they are thus analogous to properties of inanimate things or materials. But even as a mere analogy, this holds only for some types of human or animal dispositions. It is closest for those which are automatically displayed, and much less so for those which are not. Habits are dispositions, but not all habits are on a par. The habit of dining at seven is obviously not on a par with the habit of holding one's fork in the left hand and one's knife in the right, nor the habit of playing golf on Saturdays with the habit of following through in playing any shot.

"Motive," like "fear," "desire," and "hope" has a dispositional as well as an episodic or occasional sense. A motive for a particular action is what one hopes to achieve or avoid by it: hence desire and what one desires, fear and what one fears, are motives. In the dispositional sense, a motive is the disposition to act with a certain type of motive, and it is in this sense that some character traits such as vanity, curiosity, and avarice are motives. When one asks why a person did what he did, one is usually asking what his motive or motives were. The goal or aim, or the intention or intent in the sense of the intended result, are virtually the same as the motive in the sense of *what* one desires or hopes for. These notions are teleological. Stimulus-Response theory, since it claims to explain human and animal behavior, claims to be a theory of motivation, but takes motivation to be a type of efficient causation. A disposition which results from conditioning is displayed when a specific type of stimulus causes the specific type of behavior. Thus an animal that has regularly received food on pressing a lever is conditioned or motivated to press the lever when it is hungry, hunger being the internal stimulus and the lever the external or distant one. Conditioning being motivation, a disposition which results from it is a motive in the dispositional sense. Hence *in S-R theory,* the analogy with properties holds for motives.

Associationism, the mentalist ancestor of S-R theory, is by contrast primarily an account of the acquisition of expectations and beliefs. In Hume's version, and in most, these are dispositions or propensities, but merely mental ones. They are not dispositions to act and certainly not motives. For the acquisition of motives to act, pleasure and pain and the original propensity to seek the one and avoid the other are also required. Though Hume and other associationists take a motive to be a cause in their doctrines, it remains in their actual use a teleological concept, the action being explained by what the actor has in view or hopes for as a result. Stimulus-Response theory, on the other hand, is concerned just with the explanation of behavior: learning is not the acquisition of factual beliefs, far less of knowledge, but just of dispositions to behave in specific ways. Since factual (propositional) knowledge and beliefs are not motives or even dispositions, there is really no place for them in S-R theory. Since other animals have no language and hence no propositional knowledge or beliefs, this is no defect where rats or monkeys are concerned. But it is a defect where we are concerned, and for that reason alone, it is not, to say the least, a promising doctrine for the naturalization of epistemology—much less so than even associationism. Quine, like others, repeatedly falls back on the ancestral doctrine to eke out its deficiencies. But Quine's epistemology is hardly concerned with the concepts of knowledge and belief. Belief is considered chiefly in connection with so-called verbs of propositional attitude and referential opacity. Instead of knowledge and belief, we have posits and theories— sets of sentences held true. It is evident from many contexts, however, that the distinction between reasons to believe that *p,* or to hold "p" true, and motives to do so, finds no place in his doctrine, though there is of course no doubt that he makes the distinction just like anyone else when he is not professing that doctrine. Here is one example of the doctrinal confusion:

> Considered relative to our surface irritations, which exhaust our clues
> to an external world, the molecules and their extraordinary ilk are
> thus much on a par with the most ordinary physical objects. The

positing of those extraordinary things is just a vivid analogue of the positing or acknowledging of ordinary things: vivid in that the physicist audibly posits them for recognized reasons, whereas the hypothesis of ordinary things is shrouded in prehistory. Though for the archaic and unconscious hypothesis of ordinary physical objects we can no more speak of a motive than of motives for being human or mammalian, yet in point of function and survival value it and the hypothesis of molecules are alike. So much the better, of course, for the molecules.[1]

Motives are often called reasons. But as Quine and everyone well knows, the motives for thinking up a hypothesis, of which the most immediate and obvious is the desire to account for or explain some phenomena, are distinct from the reasons for accepting it or believing it to be true or on the right track. These reasons are empirical and logical and quite distinct from motives—desires, hopes, and fears. A motive is always a motive to act or to engage in some activity, whether or not one does so, but empirical factual belief is no sort of action or activity. A motive to believe that p or to hold "p" true is a motive to act as if one believed that p, but not a reason to believe that p. Though in the case of the "archaic and unconscious hypothesis," according to Quine, we cannot speak of motives, its survival value would obviously be a motive were we conscious of it, the desire to survive being certainly a motive. It follows on this account that in the case of a conscious hypothesis, we adopt or accept it for its advantage or utility for some purpose. We must of course believe, in the straightforward sense, that it *will* be useful or advantageous to act as if we believed it and there may be good reasons to believe *that*. But that is distinct from any reason to believe the hypothesis itself. It is distinct simply because advantage and utility are relative to purposes and therefore to motives and interests, and where these are concerned the first question to be asked is always "Whose?"

The notion of survival value in evolutionary biology is not relative to any purpose or interest, at least not in the Darwinian theory of natural selection or any of its now numerous revisions. Hence we cannot speak of motives. Since these theories are all purely causal, neither the value of any end, nor the value of any means to any end, enter into them. So-called survival value therefore is not really value at all, though one cannot use this undeniably apt and useful expression without at least suggesting that it is. The same goes for the notion that a trait or a type of behavior or the development of an organ confers an advantage, since advantage is advantage for a purpose, and likewise for the notion of successful adaptation, since success is success in achieving some goal. All these notions are borrowed from the human social context, where we do indeed have interests, purposes, and motives in great diversity and in frequent conflict. That they are so natural in the biological context is the reason why the argument from design seemed, and still seems to many, the most natural argument for the existence of a Higher Power: it is not always easy to keep the notion of a function distinct from that of a purpose.

Exponents of social Darwinism in its various versions take the biological contexts in which the notions of survival value, advantage, and success occur as the primary ones—metaphysically primary, one might say, though *they* never would—and applying them thence to human, social, and historical contexts, hold that natural selection will and should also work there, in so far as it is not impeded by according artificial advantages at the expense of the successful to natural failures in the struggle for existence. In its heyday, circa 1900, the idea of human eugenics based on natural selection spanned the political spectrum from the Right, especially among the exponents of rival Imperialisms, to the Left, where it was strong among the British Fabians. Though it is far from dead yet, it has on the whole got a bad name. But social Darwinism survives in forms divorced from eugenics, and in one of these forms it is part of Quine's doctrine, cultural selection being a form of natural selection.

When epistemology is naturalized in the Quinean manner, it is first psychologized in individuals with the help of S-R theory (each projecting his world) and then the jump is made by transposing the doctrine to a continuing society, though no particular one, under the name of Man, this being the individual subject writ large. Quine's naturalism does not include history, cultural anthropology, or ethnology, nor even in any serious way historical linguistics or philology. That would make things altogether too complicated. But it does include Darwinism or at least the central idea of natural selection. There is a ready-made analogy between the conditioning of individuals in S-R theory and the natural selection of random variations within a species in Darwin's theory: the variations with survival value are, so to speak, reinforced over many generations and the unfavorable ones extinguished. The myth of association and induction consorts equally well with both doctrines. Concepts, doctrines, and theories survive and flourish reinforced by advantage and success, or fade and die, extinguished by disadvantage or failure.

Quine's doctrine is a form of pragmatism, in which the criteria of truth are survival value, advantage, utility, or success. A criterion in this sense is not a necessary condition, such as the criterion of identity in Leibniz's law, nor a necessary and sufficient condition as in Alfred Tarski's criterion of truth—these are logical criteria—but a standard by which we are to judge, i.e., an epistemic criterion. Thus a common criterion of the truth of a hypothesis is coherence or consistency with known facts and with already confirmed hypotheses. If a pragmatic criterion is taken simply to be one that is employed for its advantage or utility, then any criterion should obviously be pragmatic. But advantage and utility are relative to purposes, and the question is whether the purpose is to determine truth or whether it is some other purpose. If the purpose is to establish truth, the criterion may be relevant to many purposes, since truth and knowledge are. But if it is some other purpose, that purpose will govern what we should believe, hold true, or regard as true. Let us call such a criterion heteronomic.

The criteria of truth in theology are heteronomic in this sense. What is taken to be true in theological doctrines is subordinate to the motives of faith and the purpose of salvation. Heteronomic criteria are criteria of last resort, marking the limits or bounds within which doctrinal arguments may be deployed and differences expressed. Within these bounds the usual criteria of coherence and consistency may apply. Historically, the bounds or limits marked by dogmas shift and what is within or without may be open to dispute as well of course as the interpretation of the dogmas. But whatever is taken to be the essential core of dogma and doctrine, no objection to it is to be regarded as decisive or insurmountable, as objections to merely mundane theses and theories frequently are. Thus though there is no solution to the problem of natural evils (e.g., cerebro-spinal meningitis) consistent with God's perfect goodness, it is assumed that nevertheless there must be.

The same goes for many other kinds of metaphysical doctrines, though their adepts do not recognize them to be founded on dogmas of faith, e.g., Hume's doctrine of impressions and ideas. Holding such a doctrine consists of professing it. It is both a disposition to engage in various verbal performances and the state of mind which results.

The latter is a motive in the sense of the desired result and the former a motive in the sense of the desire for that result. There may be secondary motives too and commonly there are. Those theologians who deny any conflict between faith and science, who claim that such conflicts are based on misunderstanding, and who accept the distinction between knowledge of mundane matters of fact and the dogmas of faith, are at least half-way to understanding that the criteria of truth are heteronomic in theology, but not in merely mundane matters or in science.

Exponents of other types of metaphysical doctrines, however, do not recognize this, especially when these doctrines are epistemological and least of all when they claim them to be, or to be continuous with, science. The essential dogmas on which empiricist doctrines are founded are those from which skeptical problems infallibly arise, and these problems are insoluble, as Hume recognized. It follows that all so-called knowledge of matters of fact is founded on faith, however natural or universal. How this faith arises is expounded in Hume's account of identity and of bodies as fictions. The belief in bodies is an example of perfect belief, unlike belief in God, since it is unalterable and untroubled by real doubt. But that it is faith follows from the thesis that we not only do not and cannot ever know there are bodies, we have absolutely no reason to believe there are, for the so-called belief rests on "a kind of fallacy and illusion."

Quine's doctrine of posits and of ontological commitment descends from Hume's. We do not and cannot ever absolutely know anything, all so-called knowledge is theory or language-relative, and the supposed fact that there are bodies is just "the immemorial doctrine of enduring middle-sized objects." Quine's doctrine claims to be, to be about, and to be continuous with science, but it is itself a doctrine of faith and simply projects itself on common knowledge and science. The distinction made by theologians, whose doctrines are recognized to be metaphysical, between knowledge and matters of faith, is thus effaced, and faith in the guise of commitment is foisted on matters of mundane fact. The criterion of all truth is therefore heteronomic. But it is not, and cannot, be recognized as such in the doctrine. Pragmatic criteria being the only conceivable ones, they could not conceivably be heteronomic. The distinction between advantage for establishing truth and advantage for some other purpose disappears, together with the distinction of reasons and motives.

Subordinate to the criteria of advantage are simplicity and economy in "theory building." "The neurological mechanism of the drive for simplicity," says Quine, "is undoubtedly fundamental, though unknown, and its survival value overwhelming."[2] His writings are studded with such pronouncements. It is true that people like simple theories and simple doctrines—Original Sin, associationism, monetarism, and so on. Quine himself remarks on the "looseness" of the idea of simplicity. Economy is a rather more promising idea. If we take theories to be explanatory, economy is economy of explanation, explanatory power. A theory that provides a unitary account of diverse phenomena and from which testable consequences can be inferred is more economical than a set of theories each of which would account for some but not all of the same phenomena. But the very notion that theories are explanatory assumes that there are facts (true propositions), and in the last resort facts known by observation of actual things, to be explained. In Quine's doctrine, however, no fact is thus pre-theoretical since no object is. The notion of economy, therefore, cannot be that of explanatory power but something else, and success will not be success in accounting for facts but success in something else.

If the notion of economy is not that of explanatory power, what is it? It seems to me clearly to be that of instrumental efficacy or technical rationality. In the practical contexts to which it belongs, technical rationality is relative to purposes, relative to the limits imposed by different and competing purposes and the need for accommodation of one to another, relative to means and resources, and not least relative to knowledge and available theory. Now if the purpose of formulating and testing hypotheses is to explain facts, there is no other purpose it may be accommodated to without some sacrifice to this one, and it is certainly sacrificed if we deny any fact to maintain a theory. In Quine's doctrine, however, since no fact or statement is pre-theoretical or known to be a fact just by practical experience, there cannot be recalcitrant facts, facts that are inconsistent with a theory; all there can be is inconsistency of some statements with others. Inconsistency may be obviated in various ways, indeed in any number of ways, but it ought to be obviated in the most economical and conservative way, by holding this true and holding that false according to our purposes. This is the principle employed in the construction of theological and metaphysical doctrines: they are conceptual and linguistic engineering jobs, and quite neat jobs sometimes, except for the square wheels. If this were the nature of all so-called knowledge and science, they would be in the same boat. And for Quine they are: horses, electrons, the gods of Homer, and no doubt the Holy Ghost are epistemologically on a par, "myths for working a manageable structure into the flux of experience," as he puts it in "Two Dogmas." Any statement may be held true come what may, if we make drastic enough adjustments elsewhere in the system; and, conversely, no statement is immune to revision. The model is the design and construction of a material artifact, for example a vehicle. Any factor, e.g., power, may be improved if we make adjustments of other factors—fuel consumption, speed, weight, durability, and safety. In real engineering, we have to leave some desirable features out, modify our demands in face of cost and other limits, accept trade-offs, substitute, compatibilize, and integrate. The account of theory-building in *Word and Object,* and the linguistic engineering that goes on throughout it, is a kind of verbal parody of real engineering. We decide what must be sacrificed; what can be conveniently eliminated; what can be adapted, modified or substituted; what will be economical. We redistribute truth values, gerrymander the syntax, paraphrase some "obscure" constructions, substitute others, and regiment English idioms. We even reparse proper names as predicates true of just one object. But in the end we have to settle for two vehicles—one the austere construction and the other the second-grade contraption for daily use.

> To implement an efficient algorithm of deduction is no more our concern, in these pages, than was the implementation of communication. But the simplification and clarification of logical theory to which a canonical logical notation contributes is not only algorithmic; it is also conceptual. Each reduction that we make in the variety of constituent constructions needed in building the sentences of science is a simplification in the structure of the inclusive conceptual scheme of science. Each elimination of obscure constructions or notions that we manage to achieve, by paraphrase into more lucid elements, is a clarification of the conceptual scheme of science. The same motives that impel scientists to seek ever simpler and clearer theories adequate to the subject matter of their special sciences are motives for simplification and clarification of the broader framework shared by all the sciences. Here the objective is called philosophical, because of the breadth of the framework concerned; but the motivation is the

same. The quest of a simplest, clearest overall pattern of canonical notation is not to be distinguished from a quest of ultimate categories, a limning of the most general traits of reality. Nor let it be retorted that such constructions are conventional affairs not dictated by reality; for may not the same be said of a physical theory? True, such is the nature of reality that one physical theory will get us around better than another; but similarly for canonical notations.[3]

The clarification of logical theory, as Quine understands it, is what is represented in his discussion of attributes and classes as abstract objects, of general terms as meaningful and true or false of various objects but not meaning any kind of thing, property, relation, etc., in his rejection of modality *de re,* and his complementary view of what may and may not be represented in canonical notation. His dictum that to be is to be the value of a variable merely follows from the tacit unacknowledged dogma that to be is to be an entity or particular. The only variables are individual variables; predicate letters are not variables because there are no values for them to have— no kinds, properties, actions, or what have you. It is the metaphysics that imposes all this on logic; "logical theory" is just a misnomer. What he understands by the canonical scheme in logic is complementary to the physicalist doctrine and the elimination of so-called mentalist terms. But since there is no fact of this or any other matter, we may switch Muses and use these or any terms freely, reverting to the second-grade system, whenever it suits our purpose. And why not? Technical rationality is intrinsically *ad hoc.*

It might be thought that by "theories adequate to the subject matter of their special sciences" was meant theories that accounted for or explained data or facts. But no. A simpler and clearer theory is one that is internally simpler and clearer, a better engineering job, not one that explains more than another. That is why it is not dictated by reality—it is not to be judged by the diversity of facts it accounts for. There are ultimately no facts to account for—all so-called facts are theory relative. As for "the nature of reality" according to Quine's doctrine, all we can, so to speak, know anything about is our posits. The notion of reality as independent of any belief, term, concept, or theory is the vulgar notion on which the vulgar notions of fact, or truth, and of knowledge depend; and which starts from the fact that we encounter many things, and especially people, face to face and hand to hand. Combine the posit doctrine with these vulgar notions, get the lines crossed, and we have, as Hume said of the representative doctrine, "the monstrous offspring of two principles, which are contrary to each other, which are both at once embraced by the mind, and which are mutually unable to destroy each other."[4]

When Quine is talking about science in what is ostensibly the usual modern sense that comprises physics, chemistry, and biology but not theology, astrology, fairy-lore, or witchcraft, one may forget that in his larger and looser sense of "science" or "theory" any set of beliefs and any doctrine whatever is a theory. The context in which he speaks of one theory getting us around better than another is that of physics. Yet, many doctrines get people around. The Arab conquests from the seventh to the eleventh centuries are hardly imaginable without the doctrinal faith of Islam. Unless there are determinable, knowable matters of fact in the ordinary sense, there can be no distinction between a doctrine or theory that gets us (or some of us) around because we believe it and which we therefore have a motive to believe, and one that gets us around because what we believe is true, whether or not we like it or wish it were otherwise. We may then simply hold true and hold false, in accordance with the principles of economy and simplicity within pragmatic limits, and revise or reinterpret our doctrine in the most economical and conservative way when expectations are not fulfilled (e.g., when the Second Coming does not materialize on the expected day). The rejigging, not to say jukery-pokery, is all carried out within the doctrine, since there is no such thing as a critical, external, nondoctrinal standpoint and doctrines are incomparable or, as the expression goes, "incommensurable." We change, bend, or stretch the meaning of terms and redistribute a few truth values to give the most satisfying results. In a word, we cook the books. Truth being relative to a set of terms and the language of a doctrine, the true believer may seek truth earnestly and absolutely only in the terms of his own doctrine, his own ontological commitments—that is, his faith. He can hold true and hold false whatever will serve most economically to compatibilize the essential things to which his dogmas or ideology commit him.

Real technology is not just engineering but science applied to engineering, and it is because bridges should not collapse, dams burst, or planes crash that it is important to get the theory and the calculations right. That is to say, the theories must not themselves be engineered like the artifacts—according to our motives, purposes, and desires—

as metaphysical doctrines are. The doctrine that all theories are woefully undetermined by the data belongs to empiricist metaphysics, according to which sense data—or in Quine's doctrine, the stimulations of our nerve endings (of which we know nothing in any particular case)—are all the data we ever have for anything. It follows from that doctrine that we know no more about the universe than Aristotle or even Homer. We do not even absolutely know there are horses or people, for it might turn out, as Quine and Smart agree in their charming *pas de deux,* that there are no bodies.

The notion of technical rationality is displaced from practice to theory because the notion of commitment has first migrated. Commitments in the ordinary everyday practical sense are what we have undertaken to do. Promises and contracts are moral and legal commitments. We may be committed to courses of action, policies, or strategies when we have gone too far to turn back. These are particular and more or less explicit commitments. But they arise or are made within an ethos and a framework of practices, institutions, and roles to which we are committed, by-and-large, without choice by birth, upbringing, and education, and which exist or are sustained in being by a community's practical commitment to them. The same goes of course for religions. They change as needs and interests change, in large part as a result of change in the material conditions of life. But knowledge and science are not matters of commitment: they are the results of experience and investigation. We may be committed in various ways to their advancement, but the results, whatever they are, are not matters of commitment: we cannot help knowing what we know, whatever may be our needs, motives, interests, and commitments.

If moral or social attitudes and dispositions like factual beliefs are equally the result of conditioning by positive and (so to speak) negative reinforcement, as they must of course be in S-R theory, they will likewise have survival value. And when common sense "goes self-conscious" we should expect simplicity, economy, and efficacy to govern what we hold right or wrong as it governs what we hold true or false. The fundamental criteria of truth in science and right in ethics would be the same. Scientific commitment and the distribution of truth values would be on a par with moral commitment and the distribution of positive and negative moral judgments. Moral judgments commonly depend on what are assumed to be material facts, but material facts in no way depend on moral judgments. Thus, if it is held that a type of action is wrong because it produces results that are bad, this claim may be refuted by showing that it does not in fact produce these results, whether or not it is agreed that such results would be bad or that the type of action would be wrong if it did produce them. Many moral judgments are based on false material assumptions. But people often deny material facts or tailor factual claims to save moral, and political, judgments. In Quine's doctrine it is hard to see, not only why they should not do this, but how they could fail to do it, whenever the economy of the network of reinforced dispositions demanded it. There are no known material facts in the ordinary vulgar sense: if there *were*, the position expressed in "Two Dogmas" that "no statement is immune to revision" would be simply scandalous, a license to lie. But unless there are, it is not just the concept of knowledge that goes down the drain but also that of morality—any morality.

As a factual thesis, Quine's doctrine has not a leg to stand on, but according to it, since there is no fact of any matter but in the terms of some theory, there are no legs for it or any other theory to stand on. All we can look for are the motives and advantages of this doctrine, as it invites us to do. But since it foists metaphysics on common knowledge and science and assimilates them to itself, the question we ask is not a question that could be asked by anyone who held it: for what attitudes and practices does it provide a metaphysical foundation and justification?

In metaphysical doctrines we speak of man, as if we were all pals together. Concrete questions of survival value, utility, expediency, or of what will get us around best, however, assume an answer to the questions who *we* are, how we are situated, what we want to accomplish, and where, if anywhere, we want to go. But there is a general answer to the question what gets people around or what has utility or survival value: power. Since technology (applied science) together with organizational and financial engineering became the principal factors in the production of wealth and in collective power, those who command these things—states, corporations, or individuals—have power. Technical rationality prevails in the struggle for power. This is the underlying model and the animating ideal for Quine's metaphysical doctrine of language, science, and culture. It provides his pragmatic criterion of truth and is read back into evolution itself.

Those who get around best have the best total evolving theory of reality, and since we obviously get around best, we do.

Technologies are not in fact simple outcomes of scientific discovery, and though they test theories, that is not the purpose for which they are developed. They are developed to serve material interests—principally the interests of those with the power and wealth to develop them. They are successful when they do so. Of course technology is a powerful stimulant to scientific research, but that too goes broadly in the directions for which funds are provided, ultimately by governments and enterprises with a material interest in the results. It is fair to say, as Quine does, that "science works technological wonders,"[5] since the wonders are applications of science. But it has to be added that it does not necessarily work any particular wonder, whether it be short-stalk rice or MIRVs.* Neither science nor the theoretical interests of scientists determine what wonders are to be worked, how they are to employed, in whose interest or for whose benefit (besides the interest of those who command them), and at whose expense. Science is neutral but technology is not. The idea of a fruitful theory—or in Quine's expression, the "undeniable fecundity" of science—masks two different things. Roughly, a theory is successful when it explains what it was meant to explain and stands up to tests, and it is fruitful when it explains other things as well. That it may fulfil some hopes and desires and confound others is irrelevant to its success or fruitfulness. But applied science or technology is successful when it accomplishes the purpose for which it was intended, and fruitful when it accomplishes other purposes as well. Success and fruitfulness here are entirely relative to material desires, hopes, and interests. To each of these notions of success, a cognate notion of progress corresponds. In the first case, the progress of science, the question of whose interests are served does not arise: whether one theory is better than another has nothing to do with that, nor with the use made of any discovery. The progress of science comprises any progress, any discovery, in any science. But the purpose of technology being to serve material desires and interests, its progress is relative to these, and the question of whose desires or interests are served by any technological wonder can always be raised. Quine's model of human progress is scientific progress; ostensibly the question

---

*Short for "multiple independent reentry vehicle"—a missile designed to carry many nuclear warheads.

of who benefits does not arise. But it turns out that, in his doctrine, the criterion for scientific progress and for truth is technical rationality, instrumental efficacy, what will get us around best. This is the criterion for technologies—it is technologies that get us around.

Advanced technological societies themselves have unemployable or marginal people in increasing numbers. When people speak of *us* they often ignore *them*. But *we* know who we are not: we are not citizens of tributary states under indirect rule via client regimes; not cheap labor nor the surplus people who keep it cheap; not landless peasants nor inhabitants of shanty towns, illiterate, hungry, diseased, prolific, and short-lived. No one would ascribe the plight of these losers in the struggle for existence to defects in their total evolving theory of reality. It is inimical to the spirit of metaphysical doctrines to come down to brass tacks. But social Darwinism in its largely unrecognized cultural versions, as in its more obviously pernicious genetic and racial versions, is a doctrine according to which all is for the best, progress is in the nature of things, and the plight of the losers is the price of progress.

Quine's version is one of the more sophisticated—or far-fetched— since it is a metaphysical doctrine of languages as incorporating science, concepts, and theories of the world. To accomplish this fusion or con- fusion, the distinction between concepts and terms and that between propositions (theories, theses, and beliefs) and the sentences in which they can be expressed must be rejected; translation must be indeter- minate and reference inscrutable; and bilinguals must in effect have two minds. An alien belief, doctrine, or culture is accessible only through translation of the alien language, and since translation consists of read- ing one language into the other or projecting it upon the other, the alien culture will be assimilated to our own. That we can understand or misunderstand an alien system of concepts, beliefs, attitudes, and practices and be right or wrong about them is ruled out. So worry on that score is vain. Access is translation and translation is projection. Hence we judge the alien system and are condemned to judge it by our own standards. That we often do this is of course a commonplace fact. Linguistic transcendentalism and its corollary indeterminacy of translation, however, provide a metaphysical foundation for the claim that we cannot fail to do just this.

The principal set of standards by which all societies and cultures are now in fact judged are the ones imposed by the latest stage in the development of industrial, military, and financial technology, the current set of *ad hoc* and circumstantial canons of technical rationality. The cultural conquest is accomplished by the incorporation of most countries and peoples—some as junior partners, others as menials and mendicants—in the international division of labor. In this environment, the ideas of autonomy, protection, self-defense, resistance, and revolt, since they work against and defy the environment, are maladaptive and therefore irrational. Adaptation consists essentially in learning the more successful "language."

We do not, however, have to stick to one language; we can be bilingual or multilingual, and switch Muses as the need arises. Instrumental efficacy being intrinsically *ad hoc,* why not? This again reflects the common practice of those who get around. Whatever second-grade idioms or third-rate images are required in the front shop to sell the goods (mixers or MX missiles, pop singers or politicians), in the back shop the ultimate traits of reality are limned in canonical notation, black and red. In the front shop we speak of liberty and human rights; in the back shop of power, interests, and *raison d'état.* The fundamental theory is the theory of how to get around.

NOTES

1. W. V. Quine, *Word and Object* (Cambridge, Mass.: MIT Press, 1960), p. 22.
2. Ibid., p. 20.
3. Ibid., p. 161.
4. *Treatise,* p. 215.
5. W. V. Quine, *Ontological Relativity* (New York: Columbia University Press, 1969), p. 133.

Part Three

Roots of Metaphysics

10

Knowledge and Belief, Imagination and Faith

One motive for skeptical arguments concerning common knowledge and belief was to save religion and theology from threats arising from the advance of natural science. The dogma of ideas, the immediately given, was the principal weapon in this counter-offensive. It could not itself give victory. But since any sally beyond the confines of the ideas must be, as it were, a leap of faith, traditional doctrines were to that extent restored to parity. No fact could be certainly known beyond the veil of ideas, but there were various stories or myths, spontaneous or deliberately constructed, and various motives to accept or adopt them. This position is Quine's today, though the veil is not one of ideas but of stimulations.

The effacing of the distinction between empirical knowledge and belief on the one hand and faith on the other was accomplished by blurring the distinction between perceiving and imagining. To perceive is to have ideas. To imagine is also to have ideas. Whatever is imaginable is possible, says Hume. If all so-called knowledge begins with perception, perception is still disarmed by its assimilation to imagination. To this end the distinctive characteristics of imagining must be ignored. The difference becomes a matter of degree. Degree of what? In Hume's doctrine, it is degree of belief, of the force and vivacity of the perception. Thus empirical belief and so-called common knowledge are assimilated to faith, for it is faith that is strong or weak, forceful or feeble, fervent or lukewarm.

Knowledge and belief are states, but not states of mind. But the ideal of faith is a state of mind and that state of mind is *perfect* faith, actual faith being imperfect and falling short of the ideal. Now there are some types of experience from which we have this ideal. The principal one is, I think, dreaming: dream belief provides a unique case of perfect, unquestioning, childlike faith. The incuriosity of empiricist philosophers regarding perception is excelled only by their lack of interest in dreaming. The standard doctrine of how we distinguish dreaming from waking, or know we are awake and not dreaming, is that waking experience coheres with and on the whole confirms memory and expectation. That this is not how we do in fact know we are awake, if recognized, was a matter of no importance. Dreaming or waking, we were having ideas, and *a priori* there could be no intrinsic difference between dream ideas and waking ideas.

Hume's elaborate account of imagination and belief in the *Treatise* is replaced in the first *Enquiry* by the summary notion of a "powerful natural instinct," I suppose because he realized its defects. But taken as an account of faith, it is, in my opinion, on the mark. The dogma of impressions and ideas and the skeptical problem not only permit but oblige us to speak of the belief in—or as Hume says, the belief of—perceptible things like hats and shoes and stones, as we speak of the belief in God, the Devil, Santa Claus, and fairies. Hume generally uses "faith" to mean religious belief. But for him the natural belief in body does not differ essentially but only in degree, from belief in God or the gods; that is to say, it is assimilated to faith. It is the prime if not the only example of steadfast, inalterable, fixed, and invariable faith, in comparison with which religious faith is fragile and intermittent. Of course it is not faith at all, far less the paradigm or even the ideal of faith. What Hume has done, contrary to his explicit doctrine, is to take faith as the model for the so-called natural belief. His doctrine is hopeless on hats and shoes and stones. Since we put hats and shoes on and off and lift and lay stones, it is preposterous to say we believe in them or any other material thing we come across. But his doctrine is excellent on God, the gods, and other supernatural beings. His account of belief as a sentiment or feeling and of imagination is entirely relevant to objects of faith. Only if ordinary material things were objects of faith could one speak of belief in them or regard the belief as a feeling. Liveliness, force, and vivacity have nothing to do with real objects of perception, but everything to do with the invisible and intangible objects of faith. In Hume's doctrine in the *Treatise,* however, hats and shoes and stones are objects not only of belief, understood as faith, but of much stronger belief than objects of faith properly so-called. Since this whole part of the doctrine fades out in the *Enquiry,* Hume must, I think, have seen its defects.

Hume deals both with the so-called belief in material things and with religious belief in the chapters of the *Treatise*—Book I, Pt. III, Sects. VII and VIII—in which the doctrine of belief as the liveliness of an idea is first introduced. His doctrine can be best understood if we ask what, according to it, is the difference between the belief in hats and shoes and stones and so-called facts about them, and the belief in God, angels, saints, and souls, and "facts" about them.

A lively idea or belief in a shoe is constantly connected with impressions which it resembles, and these impressions are taken to be the independently existing shoe itself. But there is no such impression in the case of supernatural objects. The belief in them is induced indirectly and artificially, whether by images and rituals or by sermons. If the imagination is sufficiently enlivened by hopes, fears, and other sentiments (judgment being but a species of sensation or sentiment), people may believe—up to a point and for the time being—in almost anything. The conflict between the conduct of many Christians and their professed beliefs, Hume accounts for by the lack of experience of anything resembling the future state—"the strongest figures are infinitely inferior to the subject"—and the absence or weakness of any causal relation between anything here below and anything there above or hereafter. Hence "the negligence of the bulk of mankind concerning their approaching condition." It is this passage that ends with the words: "I ask, if these people really believe what is inculcated on them, and what they pretend to affirm; and the answer is obviously in the negative."[1]

In the case of graven images, the material object is an object of belief by the same token as any other material thing. But this is not the object of faith. "We shadow out the objects of our faith, say they, in sensible types and images."[2] "They" refers here to Roman Catholics. Hume might have remarked that though in this case the distinction of representing and represented is supposed to be equally maintained by the learned and by the vulgar, the vulgar are often suspected of taking the graven image to be their only object and thus of being idolaters. It is not just objects of faith, however, that are "shadowed out" or represented in real pictures or sculptures. To understand that special case, we must understand the others and see what makes the difference.

If idolatry is understood to be simply the worship of a graven image or idol instead of what it represents, it seems hardly possible that there is any such thing. The statue or picture would be taken to be what it represents, and the only clear case of that is *trompe l'oeil* representation, which may actually deceive us. People know that a graven image is a material artifact, and there is no reason to suppose that worshipers cease at times to know this and take it for something else—Jesus or a saint or the Virgin and Child. The notion of a representation as something like what it represents does not take us very far. In reality, in all practical material respects, a monkey is much more like a man than a picture or statue of a man is like a man: it is a warm, breathing, moving animal. Only a certain area of a picture of a man is like a man, and that part is not strictly like a man, but at most like what a man looks like from a certain angle, at a certain distance, in a certain light, which are not, and do not vary with, the angle or distance of the picture or the light in which it is viewed. In the case of schematic drawings, it is not even like that. Of course there is some resemblance, but it is obviously more like an arrangement of matchsticks than like a man. If we look at the lines of a drawing on paper just for what they are, lines on paper, we do not even see a drawing. To get the picture we must not just look at the lines but go beyond them to what is not there at all and is not perceived at all, an imagined object. The lines serve as what Sartre called in *L'Imaginaire* an analogue of the imagined object. They are, as it were, the vehicle that conveys the imagined object.

In the case of portraits and many other pictures, we do not first look at what is really there, viz., the painted surface of the canvas. We are of course looking at it in the sense that we are standing in front of it with eyes open and directed towards it and know that what we have before us is a painted canvas. But the object—what or whom it is a picture of—is not really before us at all. This object is the one which is not present but which it brings it to mind and makes quasi-present, the imagined object, the object *in* the picture. We naturally ask, "Who is this?" meaning the man in the picture, or point to a figure in a group photograph and say, "That's Tommy" or "That's me there." We observe Descartes' face and features in Franz Hals' portrait or Hume's in Allan Ramsay's. But there is no face or features there, and we know it. There is just painted canvas. We are considering and speaking of someone who is not there, an imagined person whom the colors on canvas bring before us so that we do not look at them. This object is not the representation or picture of the person, it is the imagined person. The function of the representation or likeness is not to represent as a proxy represents or stands for something else, but to make present what is absent, not there at all, and in the cases of Hume and Descartes long dead. There is no illusion, no *trompe l'oeil*; we are not deceived. We do not take the picture for anything but a picture. We can perfectly well examine the paint or the brush work if we please.

Similarly, the function of an actor's performance of a role is not to represent or imitate the imaginary character but to make present what is not there, to incarnate him. The action of the play is indeed what is represented by real people on a real stage. But if we merely watched and listened to these real people, the time of each episode would be the time by the real clock as the place is the stage before us. But the objects and the action are not these ones here before us, but the imaginary ones; for example, Hamlet and Claudius in imaginary time at imaginary Elsinore. A performance will not work if we refuse to collaborate and just look at what is going on there before us. But we can perfectly well do this, if we please, just as we can look at the paint and brush work of a painting to see how it is done. (It is something analogous to this which I claim to be doing when I examine how metaphysical performances are done.)

We always know the people on the stage are actors performing in a play. This knowledge is not suspended. Knowledge cannot be. There is no disbelief that we have to suspend. But it is not the actor uttering the words who says he is a rogue and peasant slave, but Hamlet. It is the actors who speak the words on different nights in different theaters; but Hamlet does not say these things at different times and places. What we suspend is just our observation for itself of what is really going on in the real world on the real stage, in favor of the imaginary action made present by what is going on. We do not believe something else instead of what we in fact know. Imagination is not a variety of perception. But what is perceptible functions as the vehicle of the imaginary.

Though some things are more interesting, arresting, or delightful than others, nothing in the world is more or less real than anything else. But imagined people, actions, and situation can be so "real," or not very, or not at all, and this has nothing to do with whether or not the story or drama is about real historical people or based on real situations: everyone and everything in the fiction is imagined. What is so "real" is just what is vividly imagined—its "reality" resides in our affective response. Hamlet's feelings or emotions are imaginary, like Hamlet, but ours are not. Hume, having identified real belief with a feeling or the liveliness of an idea, was obliged to say that fiction, poetry, and drama were inferior in force and vivacity to history. But the belief that what is recounted in a story really happened, though it may excite many feelings, is not itself a feeling and has no intrinsic connection with any sentiment or feeling at all. (It is perhaps worth remarking that the "reality" of the imaginary has nothing special to do with any set of conventions, techniques, or devices that may be called "realistic.")

What makes the difference where the imaginary objects of religion are concerned? A myth, when it is a living myth, that is to say, not recognized as myth, fable, or legend, is believed. Belief in mythical or supernatural beings can be perfectly naive and spontaneous, and is often so in young children. Obviously such beliefs were prevalent long before any distinction was made between real beings and imaginary or fictitious beings. The distinction between what there is (or was) and what there is not (or was not) *at any particular time and place* is imposed by the experience of finding or failing to find, but not the distinction between what there is and what there is not absolutely—what exists and what does not exist. (There seems to be no example of the Greek verb *einai* [to be] used in this sense before Parmenides and no reason to believe that the existential sense of the corresponding verbs in other European languages is primitive or coeval with the other senses.) Until the distinction of real and imaginary beings is made, no distinction can be made between faith and empirical belief. The purpose of rituals, libations, and ceremonies can be just to honor, please, placate, or win the favor of the gods: if there is yet no question of what there is not, their existence, though undoubted, cannot even be affirmed. To polytheists, other people's gods are also gods and the question is not which are truly gods, far less whether they exist, but whether any of them are the same gods as theirs under other names. Some early Christians did not deny the existence of pagan gods but only that they were gods—according to them, they were evil spirits, possibly fallen angels. But once the distinction of the real and imaginary is made, and some beings are admitted to be imaginary, things can never be the same. The mythical beings are not encountered in the world like people and horses. Their existence may be doubted, and unlike mundane beliefs which (barring practical and technical difficulties) can be verified or falsified, belief in their existence cannot be verified here below.

The intention that animates rituals and prayers is then not just to please or win favor from the supernatural beings, but to believe in them. Faith, however, always presupposes faith: the desire to believe is already faith. One cannot in cold blood decide to believe; one can only engage in certain kinds of activity so that one shall. The intention is fulfilled, if it is, by the felt presence of God or the divine, answering to the fervor of the devotee's hopes and desires. The invisible intangible object of worship is sometimes made present through some real object, a representation that functions as its vehicle. The believer is not just imagining the supernatural object, nor is the performance of the ritual by himself or a priest a representation; he is a worshiper, suppliant, and participant in the enactment of the ritual. The important difference from merely looking at portraits is the intention to believe. The imagined object is not just imagined but an object of faith to whom prayer is addressed and worship directed: it is realized by treating it as real, by addressing to it real words and acts. (There is a parallel difference between an actor immersed in, personifying, or incarnating a character, and a medium or celebrant possessed or inspired by the spirit.) The difference between the visible and invisible, the tangible and the intangible, the mundane and the supermundane is not effaced. But after either kind of performance, theatrical or religious, people commonly have the return-to-earth experience in which the real world in contrast to the imaginary seems flat and stale. The function of some religious music is similar to that of pictures and sculptures. Music does not depict, represent, or refer, but because it does not, it can make present the invisible, intangible, and ineffable glory of God—or what you please.

Faith is a state of mind or spiritual state and there is no such waking state without the desire to believe and the activities which induce it. It is because the contrast with knowledge and empirical mundane beliefs is not abolished that it must be so and can never be perfect. As the belief is not empirically verifiable, the doubt can be stilled only by maintaining the state of mind. Perfect faith would be effortless and independent of the desire or intention to believe. It would be like dream belief, and this, I suggest, is the source or the principal source of the unattainable ideal.

Dreaming has to be distinguished not just from perception but from waking imagination. Though it is a kind of imagining, it resembles in one respect perception more than waking imagination, and this is one of the reasons not merely why it has often been thought to be significant but why it may have important effects even when it is not thought to be significant. Let us first consider the differences between perception and waking imagination.

Though we mean by "perception" any perceptual activity as well as state, perceiving in the ordinary sense is a genus of which various states are the species. "To perceive" means not to look, watch, listen, or handle, but to see, hear, feel, and so on. These are achievements or states, not actions or activities. To explain and simplify, let us take seeing. In the first important sense, seeing or sight is the ability to see and is contrasted with blindness or the prevention of seeing by external conditions such as darkness or a blindfold. In this sense, seeing or sight is the necessary condition of all the visual activities such as looking about, looking at something or for something, watching, and so on. In the second important sense, to see something is to spot it—this is the so-called success or achievement sense. And seeing something in this sense initiates seeing in the third important sense, the state sense: I spot something at a time but see it for a time. States last for a time, long or short. The state of seeing x, however, is sustained by the activities of looking at x and watching x, and the goal of these activities is to see more of x, what befalls x, what x does, and so on. Activities are signified in English by the continuous tenses— "I am watching . . . ," "I was looking at. . . ." Though "I was seeing a movie" is common enough, the activity is still that of watching it or looking at it. We see each episode only by watching it or looking and watching to see what happens next. By continuously watching we finally see or have finally seen the whole movie.[3]

Given the ability to see without gross internal defect or external impediment, by looking one will always infallibly see something or other. But whether or not one sees what one was looking for or hoped or expected to see is mainly a matter of what is there, in range and in view, to be seen. Like it or not, we must take what we get: having looked—merely looked at or also looked for—we cannot help seeing what we see. We can only help doing what we do—looking at or watching it. To say the state is passive or receptive is just to contrast it with the activities of which it is the goal or the result. A similar distinction can be made for all the species of perception—between listening (or listening for or listening to) and hearing, between handling something and feeling the shape and texture of it, between sniffing and smelling ("smelling," "tasting," and "feeling" have both the activity and the state senses).

Now a fundamental difference between perception and waking imagination (or imagining) is that imagining, whether it is visual, auditory, tactual, olfactory, or gustatory, is entirely an activity. Whereas perceptual activities like looking and listening have their fulfillment in (the states of) seeing something or hearing something, there is no corresponding state of imagining, no imaginative state. The activity of imagining is not a kind of looking or listening. The only states in which imagining results or which it enhances are affective or emotional, and the vividness or liveliness of what is imagined lies there. The objects are not given or encountered but produced and sustained, made quasi-present by the activity. Hence one can never find in the objects as imagined any more than one imagines, that is to say, one cannot find in them anything at all. Looking is to seeing, as Gilbert Ryle remarked, roughly as searching or seeking is to finding or discovery. Perception is constant discovery. But in imagining there is no finding or discovery: the objects as imagined never outrun the imagining. Things and people can surprise us in reality because we encounter them. There is no more to any imagined encounter than we are imagining. We can only imagine more and more.

We can imagine real things and people or purely imaginary things or real things and people in imaginary situations. But whether or not we imagine things as we know or believe them to be, whether we imagine real things or imaginary things, whether we imagine a future with a view to action or just let the fancy roam, is not something over and above the activity itself but intrinsic to waking imagination. It is an intentional activity and a conscious activity. That is to say, we are not just conscious of whatever it is we are imagining, but we are consciously *imagining* it, not seeing it or looking at it. To be consciously imagining something is just to be awake and aware of imagining it: we are not looking at it and we know it. Now whatever one does intentionally, one does consciously, whether one does it spontaneously or deliberately. (To do something deliberately is not just to do it intentionally but to do it of set purpose, thinking of it before one does it or attending to it as one does it.) I use "intentional" and "intentionally" in the usual sense: what one does or says intentionally is what one means to do or say as opposed to what one does or says accidentally or inadvertently, automatically or by reflex. When phenomenologists say consciousness is intentional what they mean at least is that to be conscious is always to be conscious *of* something or other. But in the ordinary sense of "intentional" this makes no sense. Consciousness in any of its senses is a state of a person. It is a person or animal that acts intentionally or consciously or whose activity is intentional or conscious, not his consciousness which is intentional. There are conscious acts or activities but no such things as acts or activities of consciousness.

Now dreaming is also a kind of imagining, but unlike waking imagination it is not intentional and not conscious. In dreaming we are conscious of what happens and happens to us in the dream, but we are not consciously dreaming and *a fortiori* not intentionally dreaming. To be consciously doing anything we must be awake and aware of it, and in the most ordinary, everyday sense of "conscious" to be conscious is to be awake while to be unconscious is to be asleep or knocked out. We know we have been dreaming by waking up, but we do not know we are dreaming *while* we are dreaming or, in other words, we do not consciously dream. If we did, we could dream what we pleased. People sometimes say they knew they were dreaming while they were dreaming, but if so they would have known they were asleep. However, it is possible to know one was sleeping only as one wakes. It is because we do not consciously dream or know we are dreaming that people quite regularly suppose that in dreaming we believe that what we dream is all really happening. A long empiricist tradition has it that the difference between dreaming and waking lies only in the coherence of waking experience. If we believed that what we dreamt was all really happening, we would of course believe we were awake. But from the fact that we do not consciously dream, it does not follow that we *believe* we are awake. In imagining things when we are awake, we are consciously imagining—we know we are not perceiving but only imagining the things. In dreaming we do not know we are not awake and not perceiving, but neither do we believe we *are*. The waking, conscious contrast of perceiving and imagining is lost.

Whereas conscious, waking imagination is free, as Hume says— we can intentionally imagine whatever we please—in dreaming, since we do not intentionally dream, we do not and cannot imagine what we please. In this respect dreaming is more like perception than waking imagination. But it is not very like it. Though we cannot perceive what we please we are free to look or not to look at anything in view. In dreaming, there is nothing like that. Dreaming is an activity as all imagining is, but it is not a conscious activity. In dreams, things happen. They do not happen in waking imagination since we consciously imagine them happening and know it. When we are awake, whatever we imagine doing intentionally we intentionally imagine doing. But not only do we not intentionally dream, we do nothing intentionally in the dream. To do anything intentionally we must do it consciously. If we acted consciously and intentionally in the dream, we could do what we pleased in the dream. But that is just what we cannot do. What we do in a dream, or dream we are doing, just happens like everything else in the dream. Dreamt action is quasi-passive action.

In waking life we continually project goals, major and minor, immediate or ulterior, and expect or anticipate a future, long-term or short-term. But in dreaming we project nothing, we expect nothing, and we anticipate nothing. Things just happen. Everything—however bizarre or surprising it may be, if one recalls the dream—is just so. Nothing is surprising. Since nothing in the dream exceeds what we are dreaming we cannot dream of what may yet happen in the dream—that would be to dream it already. Since there is no future in the dream, we do not "know" why we are doing anything—we have no motives. Everything is unquestioned and unquestionable. There is likewise no dreamt recall of the dreamt past. Only when we are awake can we recall and project. If dreams have a peculiar timelessness, as people say, it is because the dreamt past is present and there is no dreamt future. Place and identity can be equally haywire. A dreamt place can be both one place and another place; a man with whiskers can be your grandmother, or you can be helplessly watching yourself drown.

We cannot help knowing or believing what we know or believe

as a result of our experience, observation, and inquiries, and all our practical activities are conducted in the light of what we know or believe. But what we dream is not bound by what we know or believe: we can dream what is perfectly impossible and known to be impossible. Descartes says that whether he is awake or asleep, two and three still make five, but he can say this only when he is awake. We can often say what cannot be, but not what cannot be dreamt.

Since one cannot intentionally dream or do anything intentionally in a dream, nightmares can be indescribably horrible because emotion has no issue in action, not even in futile action. But dreams can also be indescribably delightful. When we say of waking experiences that we were entranced or enchanted, this is a figure of speech. It is in dreams that we are completely entranced or enchanted and this depends on the fact that in dreams we do nothing intentionally— we are not free but captive. The natural or naive view of dreams is not that they are only dreams—as in fact they are—but that one is transported out of this world, or that their "reality" is superior to that of the real world. The vividness and the felt significance, however, cannot be conveyed or explained by recounting what we dreamt: dreams fall flat in the telling. That is one reason why people want interpretations of their dreams. Since everyone has been thus entranced and knows what it is like, the wonder of the experience remains, even though what a person dreamt was perfectly childish and preposterous. Dreams are haunting. And this is quite sufficient to account for the naive belief that there is something besides all this, viz., mundane reality. Dream belief is not real belief—you cannot really believe that a mysterious man with whiskers is your grand-mother—but it is unsullied by doubt or questions, perfect and effortless. We do know what perfect childlike faith is like.

In Wordsworth's *Immortality Ode,* the passages in which he suggests that the child's "vision splendid" comes from a prior existence are merely fanciful. The prior existence is that of childhood itself— the adult's prior existence as a child—not the child's prior existence. It is not, as the metaphysics would have it, our birth that is "but a sleep and a forgetting" but our growing up. "Heaven lies *about* us in our infancy" and not, as the metaphysics would require, behind us. What is lost is the freshness and newness of things prior to familiarity, habit, and adult practicality. That is what, *in retrospect,* is like a dream. A dream is not a dream to the dreamer. It is a state of innocence, recognized as such only after the fall.

The child's vision splendid in Wordsworth's poem has no content. Of course not. The fountain light is not the light of any myth or doctrine. Anything may be apparelled in celestial light. The obstinate questionings of sense and outward things arise when the visionary gleam has fled and they are apparelled only in the light of common day. If the ideal of faith is the perfect faith of dreams or, retrospectively, the "dream" of childhood, the content is another thing. In poetic and imaginative literature we find what appears to be an endless variety of visions or imaginary worlds, of varying power to captivate, entrance, or induce the poetic faith. But metaphysical doctrines aim at something more. They implicitly claim to be rational and literally true, and when poetry is not explicitly the enemy it is at least in comparison not really serious. Commonplace empirical knowledge is not a serious obstacle to poetic faith, but it is quite the most intractable one to metaphysical faith. Metaphysical questions therefore have to be conceived in such a way that merely empirical answers will not count as answers. The doctrines constructed in answer are accordingly intellectual visions. The light is a doctrinal light. But the ideal is still the faith of the dreamer who does not know he is dreaming. This ideal is obviously unattainable in the light of common day. The shades of the prison house once fallen are never dispelled. Knowledge and the beliefs which are based upon it must therefore be transcended, circumvented, discounted, or enveloped. Epistemology is the part of metaphysics that is devoted to this, under cover of providing a foundation for knowledge, having first by skeptical arguments reduced empirical knowledge to belief. Belief having then no foundation in knowledge is reduced to the status of faith. The professed aim of dispelling the metaphysical and imaginary doubt can be nothing but the achievement of perfect faith. The essential means of dissociation from common knowledge, of screening out the light of common day, is the use of doctrinal terms. Detachment from the senses as it figures in Cartesian and other doctrinal performances is borne entirely by such devices. Whereas we really do take leave of our senses and the light of common day in dreams, the best we can manage awake is performances in doctrinal terms which have no purchase on mundane reality.

NOTES

1. *Treatise,* pp. 113-114.
2. Ibid., p. 100.
3. See Zeno Vendler, *Linguistics in Philosophy* (Ithaca, N.Y.: Cornell University Press, 1967), ch. 4, "Verbs and Times."

Bibliography

PRINCIPAL WORKS
DISCUSSED OR MENTIONED

Abbreviations of some titles are noted in square brackets.

Berkeley, George. *The Principles of Human Knowledge and Other Writings,* ed. Warnock. London: Collins-Fontana, 1962.

Carnap, Rudolf. *The Logical Syntax of Language.* London: Routledge and Kegan Paul, 1937.

Davidson, Donald, and Harman, Gilbert, eds. *Semantics of Natural Language.* New York: Humanities Press, D. Reidel, 1972.

Davidson, Donald, and Hintikka, Jaakko, eds. *Words and Objections: Essays on the work of W. V. Quine.* New York: Humanities Press, D. Reidel, 1969.

Descartes, René. *Oeuvres Philosophiques.* Ed. Ferdinand Alquié. 3 volumes. Paris: Garnier, 1963–1973.

Dummett, Michael. *Frege: Philosophy of Language.* London: Duckworth, 1973.

Eddington, Arthur S. *The Nature of the Physical World.* London: Oxford University Press, 1928.

Feigl, Herbert. *The "Mental" and the "Physical".* Minneapolis, Minn.: University of Minnesota Press, 1967.

Frege, Gottlob. *Translations from the Philosophical Writings of Gottlob Frege.* Ed. Black and Geach. London: Blackwell, 1960.

Hughes, G. E. and Cresswell, M. J. *An Introduction to Modal Logic.* London: Methuen, 1968.

191

Hume, David. *A Treatise of Human Nature.* Ed. L. A. Selby-Bigge. London: Oxford University Press, 1888. [*Treatise*]

———. *Enquiries concerning the Human Understanding and concerning the Principles of Morals.* Ed. L. A. Selby-Bigge. London: Oxford University Press, 1894. [*Enquiries*]

Kierkegaard, Søren. *Philosophical Fragments,* Trans. and ed. D. F. Swenson, N. Thulstrup, and H. V. Hong. Princeton, N.J.: Princeton University Press, 1962.

———. *Concluding Unscientific Postscript.* Trans. D. F. Swenson and W. Lowrie. Princeton, N.J.: Princeton University Press, 1941.

———. *Either-Or.* Trans. D. F. Swenson and H. A. Johnson. 2 volumes. New York: Doubleday Anchor, 1959.

Locke, John. *An Essay concerning Human Understanding.* Ed. J. W. Yolton. 2 volumes. London: Dent, 1961.

Macdonald, G. F., ed. *Perception and Identity: Essays Presented to A. J. Ayer with His Replies.* Ithaca, N.Y.: Cornell University Press, 1979.

Pascal, Blaise. *Pensées.* Ed. L. Brunschvicg. Paris: Garnier-Flammarion, 1976.

Quine, W. V. *From a Logical Point of View.* Cambridge, Mass.: Harvard University Press, 1953.

———. *Word and Object.* Cambridge, Mass.: MIT Press, 1960.

———. *Ontological Relativity and Other Essays.* New York: Columbia University Press, 1969.

———. *The Ways of Paradox.* New York: Random House, 1966.

———. *The Roots of Reference.* LaSalle, Ill.: Open Court, 1973.

Sartre, Jean-Paul. *L'Imaginaire.* Paris: Gallimard, 1948.

———. *L'Etre et le Néant.* Paris: Coll. TEL Gallimard, 1976. Originally Published 1943.

Sellars, Wilfrid. *Science, Perception and Reality.* London: Routledge and Kegan Paul, 1963.

Strawson, P. F. *Individuals.* London: Methuen, 1959.

Vendler, Zeno. *Linguistics in Philosophy.* Ithaca, N.Y.: Cornell University Press, 1967.

Index of Names

Subject Index